HEALTH CARE IN TRANSITION

DRIVING HOSPITALS TOWARDS PERFORMANCE

PRACTICAL MANAGERIAL GUIDANCE TO REACH THE "PERFECT SYMPHONY"

HEALTH CARE IN TRANSITION

Additional books and e-books in this series can be found
on Nova's website under the Series tab.

HEALTH CARE IN TRANSITION

DRIVING HOSPITALS TOWARDS PERFORMANCE

PRACTICAL MANAGERIAL GUIDANCE TO REACH THE "PERFECT SYMPHONY"

IRENE GABUTTI

Medicine & Health
New York

Copyright © 2021 by Nova Science Publishers, Inc.
DOI: https://doi.org/10.52305/DLSN5885

All rights reserved. No part of this book may be reproduced, stored in a retrieval system or transmitted in any form or by any means: electronic, electrostatic, magnetic, tape, mechanical photocopying, recording or otherwise without the written permission of the Publisher.

We have partnered with Copyright Clearance Center to make it easy for you to obtain permissions to reuse content from this publication. Simply navigate to this publication's page on Nova's website and locate the "Get Permission" button below the title description. This button is linked directly to the title's permission page on copyright.com. Alternatively, you can visit copyright.com and search by title, ISBN, or ISSN.

For further questions about using the service on copyright.com, please contact:
Copyright Clearance Center
Phone: +1-(978) 750-8400   Fax: +1-(978) 750-4470   E-mail: info@copyright.com

NOTICE TO THE READER

The Publisher has taken reasonable care in the preparation of this book, but makes no expressed or implied warranty of any kind and assumes no responsibility for any errors or omissions. No liability is assumed for incidental or consequential damages in connection with or arising out of information contained in this book. The Publisher shall not be liable for any special, consequential, or exemplary damages resulting, in whole or in part, from the readers' use of, or reliance upon, this material. Any parts of this book based on government reports are so indicated and copyright is claimed for those parts to the extent applicable to compilations of such works.

Independent verification should be sought for any data, advice or recommendations contained in this book. In addition, no responsibility is assumed by the publisher for any injury and/or damage to persons or property arising from any methods, products, instructions, ideas or otherwise contained in this publication.

This publication is designed to provide accurate and authoritative information with regard to the subject matter covered herein. It is sold with the clear understanding that the Publisher is not engaged in rendering legal or any other professional services. If legal or any other expert assistance is required, the services of a competent person should be sought. FROM A DECLARATION OF PARTICIPANTS JOINTLY ADOPTED BY A COMMITTEE OF THE AMERICAN BAR ASSOCIATION AND A COMMITTEE OF PUBLISHERS.

Additional color graphics may be available in the e-book version of this book.

Library of Congress Cataloging-in-Publication Data

Names: Gabutti, Irene, author.
Title: Driving hospitals towards performance : practical managerial
  guidance to reach the "perfect symphony" / Irene Gabutti, Adjunct
  Professor, Organization Theory and Healthcare Management, Graduate
  School of Health Economics and Management (ALTEMS), Catholic University,
  Rome Italy.
Description: New York : Nova Science Publishers, [2022] | Series: Health
  care in transition | Includes bibliographical references and index. |
Identifiers: LCCN 2021056212 (print) | LCCN 2021056213 (ebook) | ISBN
  9781685072254 (paperback) | ISBN 9781685073824 (adobe pdf)
Subjects: LCSH: Hospitals--Business management. | Health services
  administration.
Classification: LCC RA971.3 .G33 2022 (print) | LCC RA971.3 (ebook) | DDC
  362.11068--dc23/eng/20211206
LC record available at https://lccn.loc.gov/2021056212
LC ebook record available at https://lccn.loc.gov/2021056213

Published by Nova Science Publishers, Inc. † New York

This book is dedicated to my human family:
Quelpa, Cimbalina, Fantasione, Cat, Nunù.

It is also dedicated to my feline family:
Adelchi, 3Calzini, Desculpa, Tristano, Gelsomina.

CONTENTS

Preface		xi
Acknowledgments		xv
Chapter 1	Understanding the Role of Hospitals within Healthcare Systems	**1**
	Abstract	*1*
	1.1. Introduction	*1*
	1.2. Who Are the Main Providers of Healthcare Services and What Is Their Role?	*2*
	1.3. Assessing the Contribution of Hospitals to the Overall Creation of Health	*6*
	1.4. The Role of Public and Private Providers of Care Across Different Healthcare Systems	*8*
	Conclusion	*9*
	References	*10*

Contents

Chapter 2	How Are Hospitals Changing? Their Transition from Vertical to Horizontal Organizational Models	**15**
	Abstract	*15*
	2.1. Introduction	*16*
	2.2. The "Traditional" Clinical Directorate Model	*16*
	2.3. The Progressive Patient Care Model	*21*
	2.4. The Patient-Centered Approach	*23*
	2.5. Emerging Hospital Organizational Charts	*25*
	Conclusion	*27*
	References	*28*
Chapter 3	Managing a Hospital is Like Conducting an Orchestra	**33**
	Abstract	*33*
	3.1. Introduction	*34*
	3.2. The Main Dimensions of Hospital Management	*34*
	3.3. Managerial Accounting Tools	*37*
	3.4. Health Technology Management Tools	*48*
	3.5. Multiple Case Studies to Assess the Role of Hospital Contextual Factors on Technology Implementation: A Study within the European Project IMPACT HTA	*55*
	3.6. Information Communication Technology Tools	*61*
	3.7. Human Resource Management Tools	*69*
	3.8. Driving New Professional Roles through Competencies: The Experience of the Italian Federation of Hospitals and Healthcare Organizations (FIASO)	*75*
	3.9. Designing New Career Ladders in Hospital Clinic, Barcelona	*82*

	Conclusion	*84*
	References	*85*
Chapter 4	Measuring Hospital Performance	**99**
	Abstract	*99*
	4.1. Introduction	*99*
	4.2. Understanding the Dimensions of Hospital Performance	*100*
	4.3. Implementing Balanced Scorecards in Hospitals	*105*
	Conclusion	*109*
	References	*110*
Chapter 5	Seizing the "Orchestra's Symphony": Driving All Managerial Tools Towards a Common Goal	**115**
	Abstract	*115*
	5.1. Introduction	*116*
	5.2. Driving Hospitals towards Performance Through an Integrated Approach	*116*
	5.3. An Example of Managerial Effectiveness in the Implementation of Change: Has HRM Implemented the Clinical Directorate Model Effectively?	*119*
	Conclusion	*126*
	References	*127*
About the Author		**131**
Index		**133**

PREFACE

Hospitals, just like orchestras, are made up of many "instruments" which play their notes on their own, yet within a broader symphony. If even only one instrument fails in doing its part, or if the orchestra director leaves even only one of them behind, the overall symphony will just not sound right and the final performance of all will be ruined. Out of metaphor, this book is aimed at providing practical guidance to hospital managers who are called to implement complex organizational transformations. In doing so, they must necessarily consider a high number of managerial tools and dynamics which should not be overlooked. Failing in doing this, risks to negatively affect their long-term success in reaching strategic objectives.

Hospitals do not have violins, drums, and trumpets, but they do have departments, clinical wards, clinical pathways, functional units. Moreover, their professionals must carry out different activities such as assisting patients, reporting their actions, communicating and, more and more frequently, managing parts of the hospitals themselves. Not only do physicians oversee these aspects. Nurses and other clinical and non-clinical professionals are co-responsible for them, facing frequent changes in the number and types of activities they perform.

In this context, hospital managers must design organizational charts and implement them by distributing resources and responsibilities, by setting and monitoring objectives, by assessing the performance of units. They must motivate their staff and ensure an effective use of technology. Yet, although healthcare management is widely studied worldwide, it is rare to find contributions with such a broad and holistic point of view. Although each aspect and item of hospital management is key in reaching organizational success, the risk of overlooking one or more of them is high. Specifically, if management fails in directing all its tools towards its objectives, the chances of reaching outstanding performance are poor. Managerial tools must be used in an integrated and coherent way, as multiple components of a single and clear managerial strategy.

This book opens with a presentation of the role of hospitals within healthcare system. Specifically, it explores their role within networks of providers of care and how they are experiencing rapid trends of change in their organizational assets. Although each nation may present peculiarities in its healthcare system, the transformations hospitals are facing in developed countries are very similar, and they are converging towards horizontal organizational models.

The emerging design and organizational charts of hospitals are described in the second chapter. Their transition from rather rigid, vertical models (based on departments or clinical directorates) to more flat, horizontal ones (based more and more on transversal clinical pathways) is described in detail. The reasons and effects of such transformations are explained and commented.

Chapter 3 explores the set of managerial tools hospital managers should fully master to drive such change towards is objectives and reach a desirable performance. First, managerial accounting tools are assessed. The focus is not only on which tools should be used, but rather on *how* they should be used. For example, if managerial accounting tools are built around organizational units that are no longer strategic (or are not the only strategic ones) and fail in measuring new dimensions that are gaining importance within the hospital, the effect will possibly be a limited incentive to introduce and sustain desirable forms of change. Second, the role of health technologies is explored. Starting from their broad definition (which includes medical devices, equipment, drugs, procedures, etc.), the ways and circumstances in which health technologies may be truly effective in fostering performance are analyzed. Third, information Communication Technology tools constitute another major family of items that can highly affect hospital performance. Clearly, enhancing safe and effective communication flows within and outside a hospital is key. Delays in access to relevant information or incomplete or irrelevant information flows may hinder a smooth functioning of organizational activities and negatively affect performance. Finally, human resource management tools are decisive in reaching strategic objectives. These include a vast range of tools concerning all its phases (e.g., hiring, allocating, training, evaluating). A major challenge, for example, is that of implementing an effective competency modelling strategy, to guarantee the presence of the right competencies where and when they are needed. Furthermore, career pathways must be re-designed to incentivize effort which is in line with the organization's strategic objectives.

Chapter 4 addresses the issue of how to define and measure hospital performance. Many stakeholders are involved in hospital activities (e.g., patients, mangers, doctors, nurses.) and this makes it difficult to unanimously determine which facets of performance should be held crucial and with what priority. These facets are indeed numerous and are related to dimensions such as clinical outcomes, efficacy, efficiency, safety, patient- and staff- satisfaction, patient-centeredness, etc. It is therefore important to adopt evaluation tools that allow to "balance" different dimensions of hospital performance in a reliable and transparent way. In other terms, while deciding which managerial actions to implement, it is key to link them to this multi-faceted conception of performance.

The final chapter of this book is aimed at making sense of how the different managerial tools analyzed can be used to affect hospital performance, in the light of hospitals' trends of transformation. Each family of tools is inter-related with the others, and only a full understanding of their mutual effects can lead to a sustained and long-lasting overall performance. For example, a horizontal organizational chart will never reach its intended objectives if it is not supported by tailored managerial accounting tools which can detect the performance of the emerging organizational units. These managerial accounting tools (and the targets they set), however, must be coherent with the set of competencies and ambitions of professionals. Every item is inter-related and only a good orchestra director can assure a perfect overall symphony.

ACKNOWLEDGMENTS

Many people must be acknowledged for this work. The first thank you goes to Prof. Americo Cicchetti, Director of the Graduate School of Health Economics and Management (ALTMES). He is truly thanked for his mentorship, patience, and constant presence in the past twelve years. A big thank you goes to Prof. Roberto Bernabei, my life-saving anchor.

Many dear colleagues must be thanked for working with me and teaching me so much. I have found professional and personal inspiration in each one of you. Thank you to Federica Morandi, Daniele Mascia, Silvia Coretti, Valentina Iacopino, Luca Giorgio, Dina Frezza, Nicoletta Schiena, Signe Daugbjerg, Manuela Macinati, Daniele Dimonte, Maria Giovanna Di Paolo, Giacomo Frittoli, and to all my colleagues at the Catholic University in Rome.

Many thanks go to Isabella Cerquozzi, Marco and Mariagiulia Colace, Uncle Maurizio and Aunt Elisabetta, Doina Alexandru and Olimpia Herciu. Thank you also to Elisabetta Pizzi, Luigi Janiri and Stefano Zamboni.

Finally, so much gratitude goes to the pillars of my life: my parents, my brother (who is also thanked for his precious revision of this book), Nuno, Mimmo, and my uncountable relatives and friends who sustain me day after day.

This work is for you all!

Chapter 1

UNDERSTANDING THE ROLE OF HOSPITALS WITHIN HEALTHCARE SYSTEMS

ABSTRACT

Hospitals are actors within a network of providers and their activities should not be planned, implemented, and evaluated as isolated monads, but rather in an integrated and cooperative way. Their mission is to *contribute* to the creation of health, together with other healthcare providers involved in non-acute phases of diseases. The provision of fragmented care is one of the major risks of modern healthcare systems, and this must be reduced as much as possible by designing integrated organizational models within and across healthcare organizations. Not only organizational models, but also all managerial interventions must be oriented towards the provision of integrated care.

Keywords: hospitals, primary care, secondary and tertiary care, healthcare systems, integrated care.

1.1. INTRODUCTION

Healthcare systems around the world present different features but are all characterized by the presence of multiple providers of care.

Hospitals are pivotal in these systems due to their central role in the provision of care in the acute phases of diseases. Nevertheless, the changing epidemiological features of the populations of developed countries are more and more stressing the need of "balancing" the role of hospitals with that of other providers. This means that all healthcare organizations, including hospitals, must by now be managed in an integrated way, within an organized network of providers.

1.2. WHO ARE THE MAIN PROVIDERS OF HEALTHCARE SERVICES AND WHAT IS THEIR ROLE?

Healthcare systems around the world differ under many aspects. They may be organized, managed, and financed in different ways, according to various priorities, principles, and organizational frameworks. Nevertheless, no matter which country we look at, healthcare systems usually face similar challenges and must respond through common strategies.

Populations of developed countries are generally ageing and are frequently characterized by multi-pathological chronic health issues (Tinker 2002). Patients, however, are more and more informed about their rights and their expectations are rising considerably. At the same time, however, there exist dramatic financial pressures which require healthcare organizations to provide more and better services with equal (if not decreasing) resources (Saviano et al. 2018). Therefore, many features of healthcare systems are doomed to change if these are to remain sustainable in time. Whether financed by public or private entities (or both), healthcare organizations are in fact frequently required to increase their productivity (i.e., the quantity and quality of the services they provide), while limiting if not reducing the costs they bear to do so (AlJaberi, Hussain, and Drake 2017). This means that outstanding levels of performance must be reached while implementing new, *sustainable* ways of doing so. Indeed, as will be explored in a further section of this book, the mere concept of hospital performance is multi-faceted and must take into account dimensions such as, among others, quality, efficiency, equity, and appropriateness.

Providing healthcare services is a complex challenge which must be faced by different types of providers of care and of professionals simultaneously (Mazor et al. 2016). Simplifying a possibly more complex scenario, providers of care generally belong to one of two possible families: primary care providers and secondary/tertiary care ones. The first are responsible for assisting the population in non-acute phases of their disease by, for example, taking in charge chronic patients in need of continuous monitoring or adjustments of treatment (Glynn et al. 2011). Secondary and tertiary settings such as hospitals, on the other hand, are responsible for managing acuity by usually admitting patients for at least a few days within their structures (Schang et al. 2019). Although this dichotomy may at times be disregarded (hospitals may provide ambulatory care and acute patients may be treated in settings different from hospitals), it is potentially dangerous to confuse the role of each. This is because providing health is very expensive, and this is even more the case when providing it in hospitals. In other words, the risk of providing health services in inappropriate settings may have deleterious consequences both on their quality as well as on their sustainability in the long run (Ballotari et al. 2019). This translates, ultimately, to negative consequences for the overall health of the population. Although literature testifies the tendency of patients to consider hospitals the "best place to be" if they are sick (Ward et al. 2015), this is not exactly true. Indeed, many situations can be dealt with just as effectively (or even more effectively) in primary care settings, which are usually easier to access, freeing up resources in hospitals for those patients who are truly in need of them (i.e., in an acute phase of their disease). In particular, the overall orientation is that only those activities that cannot be safely and effectively carried out in ambulatory or primary/domestic care settings should be left to hospitals. The objective is to avoid expensive inappropriate hospital admissions because of the lack of availability of services in primary care settings. Many countries, indeed, are facing phenomena of hospital reconversion to primary care settings, thereby often reducing the number of available hospital beds (Okasha 2019). This, however, should ideally not translate into a worsening of the services provided to citizens, but rather into an increased appropriateness of settings, oriented to the provision of quality and sustainable services.

Equal attention must be paid to the idea of appropriateness *within* hospitals (Apolone et al. 1997; Bianco et al. 2002). Not all settings within hospitals are the same. For example, hospitals may provide services in ambulatory settings, in day hospital[1], in day surgery[2], in week hospital[3], in week surgery[4] or, of course, in wards based on regular patient admissions (Gabutti and Cicchetti 2017). These too may be diversified based on their expected length. Assigning patients to the "right" (i.e., less expensive but equally effective) hospital setting is key in overall successful management of the organization. A formal list of activities to be carried out in day hospital and not through regular hospital admissions is frequently provided either by hospitals themselves, or by public regional or national authorities (Signorelli et al. 2020). The same should be done for those services ideally provided in ambulatory settings rather than in day hospital. Medical records of services which are at high risk of being provided in inappropriate settings should be monitored systematically and should be used to swiftly detect systematic misuse of settings. Such managerial proactivity is one of the tools to reduce the risk of incurring rooted praxes that are counter-productive for the overall success of the hospital.

If we reason in these terms, it is easy to see how a healthcare system should be thought of as a group of different providers who *jointly* provide assistance and care (Cumming 2011). Some of these should intervene in some cases, others in other ones. The role of each should be well-defined

---

[1] These are hospital admissions in which patients are treated within the day and are discharged before night.
[2] These are hospital admissions in which patients are treated surgically within the day and are discharged before night.
[3] These are hospital admissions in which patients are treated within the week and are discharged before the weekend. They usually are on Mondays or Tuesdays.
[4] These are hospital admissions in which patients are treated surgically within the week and are discharged before the weekend. They usually are on Mondays or Tuesdays.

and respected. Nevertheless, defining clear roles does not at all imply that they should be seen as independent from each other. Quite on the contrary, roles (both in terms of individual professionals and of different healthcare settings) must be integrated and oriented towards common objectives. This is where the metaphor of an orchestra comes in help. Managers in the healthcare sector (and, as we will discuss, hospital managers specifically), must be aware of the multitude of roles involved in providing care and must pursue an overall "harmonious" coherence in carrying out their activities. Indeed, each one of them must tend towards the common objective of preserving or improving the health of patients, possibly in a system-wide perspective rather than by focusing on specific, isolated interventions (González-Ortiz et al. 2018).

In other words, one of the major issues healthcare systems are facing in our era is the risk of pursuing *fragmented care*. This expression is used to describe the risk of supplying health services that are poorly linked to each other, leading to a systematic failure in "following" patients along their continuum of care (Stoop et al. 2020). Providing "parts" of assistance in a poorly harmonized way is highly problematic. This holds true especially for the high share of patients that are affected by multiple and/or chronic pathologies, who are therefore in need of a clear and organized *set* of interventions in time. Fragmented care, in turn, implies a fragmented vision of a healthcare system. If fragmentation prevails, health services are provided through disjoint interventions, each of which is likely to ascribe faults to the other links of the chain. Therefore, integrated care (or "patient-centered care", as we shall call it in the rest of this book), is closely related to the concept of performance (Sauto Arce et al. 2019; Zhong, Liang, and Yan 2018). The latter should more and more be ascribable to the health system in general (or to its local articulations), rather than to a specific setting or to a specific hospital or, even worse, to a specific professional. Although reliable assessments of individual settings (e.g., of a hospital, of one of its internal units) is key in managing an organization effectively, this must necessarily be contextualized in terms of its contribution to *overall performance*, based on the success of the overall set of services built around interventions offered to patients in time.

1.3. Assessing the Contribution of Hospitals to the Overall Creation of Health

Thinking of hospitals as one of the actors in a broader network is necessary, on one hand, to pursue an effective and efficient overall provision of care but, on the other, is likely to lead to challenges in the assessment of their concrete contribution to final outcomes. Indeed, shared responsibility is a challenging topic given that it implies not only shared missions and strategies, but also a shared assessment of performance and of success. This issue has strong implications and risks, leading to unbearable conflicts if not managed in an effective way. Chapter 4 is dedicated to the assessment of hospital performance, but it is already worth mentioning here that healthcare systems must necessarily invest in the creation of a coordinated and coherent managerial approach. For example, conceiving the healthcare system as a long list of activities or services to be carried out by specific providers of care is less and less likely to be an effective approach in the future. As mentioned, this approach is likely to nurture a fragmented vision of the national (or regional) health service and may fail in grasping the contribution of each to the concrete change in a population's overall status of health. At the same time, though, a mere assessment of overall final outcomes, intended as the overall health of people, is somewhat limiting insofar as it may fail in relating specific effects to specific efforts and actions. Moreover, this would fail in taking into due account various confounding factors which may affect health independently from the intervention of the healthcare system.

A reasonable compromise between these two extreme approaches may be that of assessing the provision of care through clinical pathways (described in Chapter 2). These should not be thought of as the mere "structure" of a process of cure. Rather, they should be conceived as a multi-faceted tool to implement a patient-centered approach, improving the quality, efficiency and sustainability of the services provided (Trimarchi et al. 2021; Aspland, Gartner, and Harper 2021). In this way, evaluating the performance of a healthcare system, or also of a specific component of it (e.g., of a hospital), should possibly consist in measuring the effectiveness of the implementation of a pathway. Its full and effective implementation, which may rely upon different organizations simultaneously, adds a further fundamental dimension to the "typical" set of performance indicators. For example, taking into account a hospital's capability of implementing clinical pathways leads to a concrete understanding of its ability of cooperating with the other actors of its network in an inter-organizational perspective. Building further on this reasoning, the joint contribution of hospitals and of other settings in the achievement of high outcomes, is likely to be more and more valued by joint forms of compensation. Many countries are adopting compensation or reimbursement strategies that integrate traditional fee-per-service approaches with new bundled payments (Dummit et al. 2016; Navathe et al. 2017). These may be referred to a single organization, insofar as their bundled nature concerns the joint effort of different units, or they may be referred to more than one organization, in all of those (frequent) circumstances in which they share a joint responsibility over the success of their common efforts.

It may be tempting to assume that the relevant differences across healthcare systems across the world may limit the generalizability of the trends of change or of new managerial approaches in the hospital sector. Although this may indeed hold true to some extent, the global features of our society highlight a surprisingly similar scenario in most of the developed world. Similar epidemiological trends, technological innovations, patients' expectations but also similar challenges in the intent of providing high quality yet sustainable health services, have led most developed countries towards the adoption of incredibly similar managerial strategies. Nevertheless, although this book is built on joint evidence coming from different nations with different healthcare systems, it may be useful to quickly recall some of the main characterizing features of the main healthcare systems of developed countries. This is briefly done in Box 1, which also describes the different roles private and public providers of care may assume within their healthcare system.

1.4. THE ROLE OF PUBLIC AND PRIVATE PROVIDERS OF CARE ACROSS DIFFERENT HEALTHCARE SYSTEMS

Health care systems in different parts of the world have evolved in different ways (Lameire, Joffe, and Wiedemann 1999). Overall, three main models have emerged in time. The first is the liberal model, present in the USA, in which healthcare services are considered in a very similar vein to other goods and services on the market (e.g., consumer goods). Public authorities intervene to concede authorizations and licenses, while it is mainly up to patients to pay for the services they buy. Large parts of the population are covered in (some of) their healthcare expenditures either by private insurances (usually provided by employers) or by federal insurance or assistance programs (i.e., Medicare and Medicaid). Prices are freely negotiated between providers and payors. Providers are nearly entirely private, with a marginal role for public ones.

The second model is the mutualistic one (Bismarck model). This is present in countries such as France, Germany, and The Netherlands. Health assistance is considered a right of citizens within the limits of social security coverage. The central state intervenes with a general regulatory framework, while management of the system is decentralized at the regional level. Services are co-financed by employers and workers and negotiation occurs between regions and providers of care. Providers are in part public and in part private.

Finally, the third model is the universalistic one (Beveridge model). This is present in the United Kingdom, Italy, Spain, and in Scandinavian countries. Access to healthcare services is guaranteed by the State. The central state is responsible for defining general strategic and planning orientations, while regions are more and more autonomous in the actual management of their local healthcare system. Services are financed through taxation. Providers are financed through pre-determined global annual budgets set by regions. Providers are mainly public and most private ones operate on behalf of the public system (following the same rules of financing of the public ones).

Although the scenarios in which providers operate vary widely across nations, the roles hospitals and primary settings should cover are not altered. Assisting patients in appropriate settings is a common goal, whether these are private or public, given that this is the key challenge in reaching an overall effective and efficient health system. In other terms, no matter what the ownership is, the roles of the different settings should be designed coherently within the overall system so as to guarantee the provision of services in appropriate settings, without wasting resources or using them in non-optimal ways.

CONCLUSION

Although hospitals play a central role in healthcare systems and within the network of providers that characterize them, their role cannot be isolated from the rest of this network. If this is done, the risk is to incur into suboptimal solutions both in terms of the quality of the services provided and of the overall sustainability of the system. This means that forms of "internal" (of the hospital) management must be combined with forms of "shared" (with the network) management. The most remarkable example of this shared perspective is possibly referable to the actual meaning of hospital performance. This is indeed built upon a series of internal performance dimensions but cannot disregard the hospital's ability to contribute to a shared effort. This need of balancing an internal and an external point of view is one of the guiding principles of the rest of this book.

REFERENCES

AlJaberi, O. A., Hussain M., and Drake P. R. 2017. "A Framework for Measuring Sustainability in Healthcare Systems." *International Journal of Healthcare Management*, 13:4, 276-285, doi: 10.1080/20479700.2017.1404710.

Apolone, G., Fellin, G., Tampieri, A., Bonanoni, E., Crosti, P. F., Lanzi, E., Meregalli, G., Trocino, G., and Liberati, A. 1997. "Appropriateness of Hospital Use Report from an Italian Study." *European Journal of Public Health* 7 (1): 34–39. https://doi.org/10.1093/EURPUB/7.1.34.

Aspland, E., Gartner, D., and Harper, P. 2021. "Clinical Pathway Modelling: A Literature Review." *Health Systems* 10 (1): 1–23. https://doi.org/10.1080/20476965.2019.1652547.

Ballotari, P., Venturelli, F., Manicardi, V., Vicentini, M., Ferrari, F., Greci, M., Maiorana, M., and Rossi, P. G. 2019. "Determinants of Inappropriate Setting Allocation in the Care of Patients with Type 2 Diabetes: A Population-Based Study in Reggio Emilia Province." *Plos One* 14 (7): e0219965. https://doi.org/10.1371/JOURNAL.PONE.0219965.

Bianco, A., Foresta, M. R., Greco, M. A., Teti, V., and Angelillo, I. F. 2002. "Appropriate and Inappropriate Use of Day-Hospital Care in Italy." *Public Health* 116 (6): 368–73. https://doi.org/10.1038/SJ.PH.1900853.

Cumming, J. M. 2011. "Integrated Care in New Zealand." *International Journal of Integrated Care* 11 (5): 1–13. https://doi.org/10.5334/ijic.678.

Dummit, L. A., Kahvecioglu, D., Marrufo, G., Rajkumar, R., Marshall, J., Tan, E., Press, M. J. et al. 2016. "Association between Hospital Participation in a Medicare Bundled Payment Initiative and Payments and Quality Outcomes for Lower Extremity Joint Replacement Episodes." *JAMA - Journal of the American Medical Association* 316 (12): 1267–78. https://doi.org/10.1001/jama.2016.12717.

Gabutti, I., and Cicchetti A. 2017. "Translating Strategy into Practice: A Tool to Understand Organizational Change in a Spanish University Hospital. An in-Depth Analysis in Hospital Clinic." *International Journal of Healthcare Management* 13 (2): 142–55. https://doi.org/10.1080/20479700.2017.1336837.

Glynn, L. G., Valderas, J. M., Healy, P., Burke, E., Newell, J., Gillespie, P., and Murphy, A. W. 2011. "The Prevalence of Multimorbidity in Primary Care and Its Effect on Health Care Utilization and Cost." *Family Practice* 28 (5): 516–23. https://doi.org/10.1093/FAMPRA/CMR013.

González-Ortiz, L. G., Calciolari, S., Goodwin, N. and Stein, V. 2018. "The Core Dimensions of Integrated Care: A Literature Review to Support the Development of a Comprehensive Framework for Implementing Integrated Care." *International Journal of Integrated Care* 18 (3): 1–12. https://doi.org/10.5334/ijic.4198.

Lameire, N., Joffe, P., and Wiedemann, M. 1999. "Healthcare Systems - An International Review: An Overview." *Nephrology Dialysis Transplantation* 14 (SUPPL. 6): 3–9. https://doi.org/10.1093/ndt/14.suppl_6.3.

Mazor, K., Roblin, D. W., Greene, S. M., Fouayzi, H., and Gallagher, T. H. 2016. "Primary Care Physicians' Willingness to Disclose Oncology Errors Involving Multiple Providers to Patients." *BMJ Quality & Safety* 25 (10): 787–95. https://doi.org/10.1136/BMJQS-2015-004353.

Navathe, A. S., Troxel, A. B., Liao, J. M., Nan, N., Zhu, J., Zhong, W., and Emanuel, E. J. 2017. "Cost of Joint Replacement Using Bundled Payment Models." *JAMA Internal Medicine* 177 (2): 214–22. https://doi.org/10.1001/jamainternmed.2016.8263.

Okasha, A. 2019. *Resource Partitioning and Hospital Specialization.* Https://Doi.Org/10.1177/0972063419868543 21 (3): 337–50. https://doi.org/10.1177/0972063419868543.

Sauto Arce, R., Lamiquiz Linares, E. M., López Arbeloa, G., Pérez Irazusta, I., Alkiza Eizagirre, M. E., and Ruiz Fernandez, R. M. 2019. "Analysis of a Scoreboard of Quantitative Indicators to Assess the

Performance on Integrated Care in the Basque Health System." *International Journal of Integrated Care* 19 (4): 358. https://doi.org/10.5334/ijic.s3358.

Saviano, M., Bassano, C., Piciocchi, P., Di Nauta, P., and Lettieri, M. 2018. "Monitoring Viability and Sustainability in Healthcare Organizations." *Sustainability 2018, Vol. 10, Page 3548* 10 (10): 3548. https://doi.org/10.3390/SU10103548.

Schang, L., Koller, D., Franke, S., and Sundmacher, L. 2019. "Exploring the Role of Hospitals and Office-Based Physicians in Timely Provision of Statins Following Acute Myocardial Infarction: A Secondary Analysis of a Nationwide Cohort Using Cross-Classified Multilevel Models." *BMJ Open* 9 (10): e030272. https://doi.org/10.1136/BMJOPEN-2019-030272.

Signorelli, C., Odone, A., Oradini-Alacreu, A., and Pelissero, G. 2020. "Universal Health Coverage in Italy: Lights and Shades of the Italian National Health Service Which Celebrated Its 40th Anniversary." *Health Policy* 124 (1): 69–74. https://doi.org/10.1016/j.healthpol.2019.11.002.

Stoop, A., Lette, M., Ambugo, E. A., Wirrmann Gadsby, E., Goodwin, N., Macinnes, J., Minkman, M., et al. 2020. "Improving Person-Centredness in Integrated Care for Older People: Experiences from Thirteen Integrated Care Sites in Europe." *International Journal of Integrated Care* 20 (2): 1–16. https://doi.org/10.5334/IJIC.5427.

Tinker, A. 2002. "The Social Implications of an Ageing Population." *Mechanisms of Ageing and Development* 123 (7): 729–35. https://doi.org/10.1016/S0047-6374(01)00418-3.

Trimarchi, L., Caruso, R., Magon, G., Odone, A., and Arrigoni, C. 2021. "Clinical Pathways and Patient-Related Outcomes in Hospital-Based Settings: A Systematic Review and Meta-Analysis of Randomized Controlled Trials." *Acta Biomedica* 92 (1): 1–13. https://doi.org/10.23750/abm.v92i1.10639.

Ward, P.R., Rokkas, P., Cenko, C., Pulvirenti, M., Dean, N., Carney, S., Brown, P., Calnan, M., and Meyer, S. 2015. "A Qualitative Study of Patient (Dis)Trust in Public and Private Hospitals: The Importance of Choice and Pragmatic Acceptance for Trust Considerations in South Australia." *BMC Health Services Research 2015 15:1* 15 (1): 1–12. https://doi.org/10.1186/S12913-015-0967-0.

Zhong, L., Liang, Z., and Yan, Z. 2018. "Current Performance and Future Trends of Integrated Care: A Scientometric Analysis." *International Journal of Integrated Care* 18 (s1): 112. https://doi.org/10.5334/ijic.s1112.

Chapter 2

HOW ARE HOSPITALS CHANGING? THEIR TRANSITION FROM VERTICAL TO HORIZONTAL ORGANIZATIONAL MODELS

ABSTRACT

Hospital organizational models are more and more based on transversal clinical pathways, changing how responsibilities are assigned and how activities are carried out. Transversality must not only be intended across hospital departments, but also across different health organizations and at the wider system level. Hospitals have traditionally shifted from models based on clinical directorates to horizontal (or matrix-shaped) organizational models. The latter have integrated "traditional" vertical responsibility centers with transversal settings aimed at "following" patients across their continuum of care. Nowadays, hospitals are frequently characterized by complex organizational charts and must face the challenge of driving their organizational transitions effectively.

Keywords: organizational models, organizational charts, clinical directorate model, progressive patient care model, patient-centered model

2.1. Introduction

Hospitals across the world have historically experienced similar transitions in their organizational configurations, in line with the main challenges and pressures coming from the external environment. After a period of highly centralized models, during the 90s many hospitals have experienced deep transformations in their organizational charts. These have gradually increased the autonomy of units in lower levels of the hierarchy and have led to a greater accountability of middle-managerial roles. Nevertheless, although this tendency to decentralize has strongly supported hospitals in facing the challenges they met in the 90s, new challenges have emerged in the meanwhile. Consequently, hospitals have experienced further organizational transformations aimed at "connecting" them with the other actors of their network in a structured way. Emerging organizational models are of great help in the management of chronicity and of multi-pathological patients yet require deep coordination abilities within and across organizations.

2.2. The "Traditional" Clinical Directorate Model

Ever since the last decades of the past century, the application of New Public Management (Simonet 2014; Caffrey, Ferlie, and McKevitt 2019; Andrews, Beynon, and McDermott 2019) principles to the healthcare sector has implied a frequent adoption of the clinical directorate model within hospitals. New Public Management was mainly aimed at modernizing managerial approaches in the public sector by implementing managerial strategies and tools borrowed from the private industry. This is because many public administrations worldwide were felt to have become too large and rigid, stiffened by an excessive bureaucracy which often compromised the attainment of effectiveness and efficiency while pursuing the organizations' activities (Moresi-Izzo, Bankauskaite, and Gericke 2010).

Organizational rigidity and innovative managerial responses through the spread of New Public Management have been two characterizing features of healthcare organizations in general, and of hospitals in particular (Mei and Kirkpatrick 2019). This is possibly so because of the high complexity of hospitals and of the crucial role they play within our societies. In this scenario, the need to overcome highly centralized, bureaucratic, and rigid organizational charts has led, ever since the 1980s, to the spread of the clinical directorate model (Gabutti and Morandi 2018). This organizational model was introduced at first in the United States but has then quickly become the major organizational response to hospital managerial challenges in most developed countries. Clinical directorates (or departments) are semiautonomous hospital divisional units in which several clinical wards are integrated or merged (Braithwaite et al. 2006; Lega 2008). Although wards may be aggregated following different criteria (e.g., specialistic medical area, nosological criteria, age of patients), the main intent of the model is to assign a high degree of autonomy and of responsibility to the hospital's sub-units (the clinical directorates), so as to make them fully accountable for their own activities. The intent of increasing their accountability implies, in turn, an increased accountability of the whole organization. This is because clinical directorates are highly empowered to pursue both effectiveness and efficiency through their activities, by exerting a high degree of control over the resources they are assigned with.

The clinical directorate model has important managerial implications at the organizational level. Clinical directors (also known as Heads of departments) cover an intermediate managerial role between top management on one side and clinical wards on the other. Top management can now focus on setting strategic plans and monitoring their implementation and achievement in time, while delegating operational activities to clinical directorates (Mascia, Morandi, and Cicchetti 2014). The latter, however, are directly responsible for the achievement (or missed achievement) of the strategic objectives set by top management. As mentioned, this responsibility is concrete given that it comes along with the direct assignment of costly resources, going from a yearly budget, to physical spaces, beds, operating rooms, technology, and staff. What emerges, therefore, are non-bureaucratic, highly decentralized hospitals. The reduced bureaucracy is due to the lower need of involving higher hierarchical tiers in many processes and decisions, which are now directly taken by departments. Their success in effectively using the resources they are assigned and in reaching their objectives will, in turn, set the bases for their negotiation power and determine the relevance of their own role within the hospital. Figure 1 shows a representation of the typical clinical directorate model within hospitals.

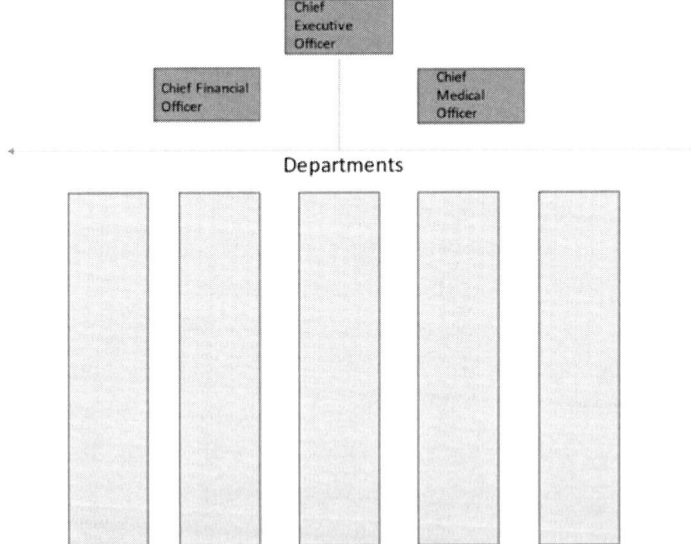

Source: Author's elaboration.

Figure 1. The clinical directorate organizational model.

This model was expected to achieve outstanding results across a range of dimensions, ranging from the clinical, to the financial, to the organizational one (Mascia, Morandi, and Cicchetti 2014). For example, it was expected that assigning resources to clinical directorates would develop very high specialistic expertise, thus positively affecting clinical outcomes. Moreover, it was expected that the delegation of responsibility to them and their increased accountability, would indeed imply a responsible use and management of resources, hence positively affecting economic/financial dimensions. Finally, in organizational terms, dividing very large organizations into smaller responsibility centers with a high degree of autonomy, was expected to result in more effective and efficient organizational solutions than those arisen with highly centralized organizational models. Whether the model has been successful in reaching its various objectives is an open debate (Gabutti, Mascia, and Cicchetti 2017). It probably has been of great help in pursuing effectiveness and sustainability in an era of increasing expectations and limited available resources (Correia and Denis 2016). In some areas of the world, it has been made mandatory for hospitals to adopt it (Gabutti and Morandi 2018), thus contributing to a deep transformation of the hospital sector in general. Nevertheless, the model has, in time, revealed some of its limits, especially if referred to the changing external environment. In the first place, its vertical organizational chart has caused sub-optimal uses of scarce and costly resources (Lega 2008). Although intended to overcome organizational rigidity, the model has introduced a new form of rigidity caused by the clinical directorates themselves. These have tended to operate in rather isolated ways with, at times, a poor coordination with other clinical directorates or other units of the hospital. For example, bed management, staff allocation as well as the use of technologies, may incur forms of waste in all those situations in which they do not reach high rates of saturation at the hospital level. A costly example is given by operating rooms. If these are managed by clinical directorates autonomously, this may lead to unassigned time slots with negative effects in terms of waiting lists and overall hospital costs. This and other resources of the hospital may be used in accountable ways by the clinical directorate, but in sub-optimal ways at the overall hospital level. A second example is related to beds. A clinical directorate may be temporarily under low pressure in terms of patient admission or may even have free beds in some moments of the week. This, however, can occur in a moment in which other clinical directorates are increasing their waiting lists because they are completely full and unable to admit other patients. If this is the case, clinical directorate accountability does not guarantee an efficient use of resources at the hospital level, possibly leading to sub-optimal outcomes.

In the second place, a relevant limit of this model is related, as mentioned, to the changing features of our social environment. An ageing population implies that the patients admitted to a hospital are typically advanced in age, multi-pathological and with chronic conditions. Therefore, even though the healthcare system is effective in assuring the access to appropriate settings of care (thus admitting in hospitals only patients in an acute phase of their pathology), it is generally unlikely that patients will find a complete response to their needs within a single clinical directorate (Braithwaite et al. 2005). This is because their multi-pathological conditions are likely to require interventions of professionals belonging to different clinical specialties. A structural design based on clinical directorates only, is likely to require continuous forms of lateral coordination and frequent inter-directorate consultancies in every-day activities. Although feasible in the short run, this organizational solution may appear inadequate in systematic terms. Frequent *ad hoc* inter-department consultations are bound to produce confusion, deviations from pre-determined procedures and, in general, inefficiencies. We can think of this model as built around the clinical specialties rather than around the patient. In other words, this "department-centric" configuration fails in "following" patients across their continuum of care (Bokhour et al. 2018). This holds true both in relation to patients' pathways within the hospital as well as across different settings in a long-term perspective.

In short, although highly effective in adapting some of the typical principles of the New Public Management stream to the healthcare sector, the clinical directorate model has possibly revealed its limits in its inability to pursue "patient-centered" care through the adoption of organizational solutions that accompany patients across their continuum of care.

2.3. THE PROGRESSIVE PATIENT CARE MODEL

As mentioned previously, hospitals have had to re-consider their design and structure due to the changing challenges they have faced in time. Gradually, new organizational forms which overcome the widely adopted clinical directorate model have emerged. In the past decade, new horizontal and transversal models have gradually integrated (if not replaced) those configurations that have prevailed previously. Different labels have been used to name such models. "Progressive patient care model", "comprehensive critical care model", "intensity of care model", "care-focused organizations" (Gabutti and Cicchetti 2017) are all expressions that, although at times applicable to different contexts and possibly different in some ways, ultimately lead back to one basic idea: pooling patients and organizing patient-flows around the acuity of patients' conditions and not around the specialty they are concerned with. Hospitals can no longer afford functional self-referential designs, where economies of scale are not exploited, resources are duplicated, clinical integration and clinical governance is nonexistent, and autonomy (in using the specialty's resources) prevails over overall efficiency (Villa, Barbieri, and Lega 2009). This implies the integration of different specialties in using fixed and shared resources, such as operating rooms, equipment, beds, staff. Literature highlights how older models have frequently caused inefficiencies in staff utilization, high rates of delay, cancellation of clinical procedures and waste of resources resulting from poor communication among departments and disciplines (Mintzberg 1997; Norrish and Rundall 2001; Lega 2007).

Therefore, in a progressive patient care perspective, patient pooling is conducted based on the degree of assistance the patient needs or on the expected length of his/her stay in the hospital. This, in turn, implies that units are now merged based on requirements of care and potential economies of scale (and no longer, as done previously, following specialty criteria only), while sharing resources across different specialties. Finally, a fundamental change introduced with the new model has to do with a new way of conceiving work, with assistance carried out by multi-disciplinary as well as multi-professional teams, with nurses generally assuming new managerial and coordination responsibilities (Colamesta et al. 2018).

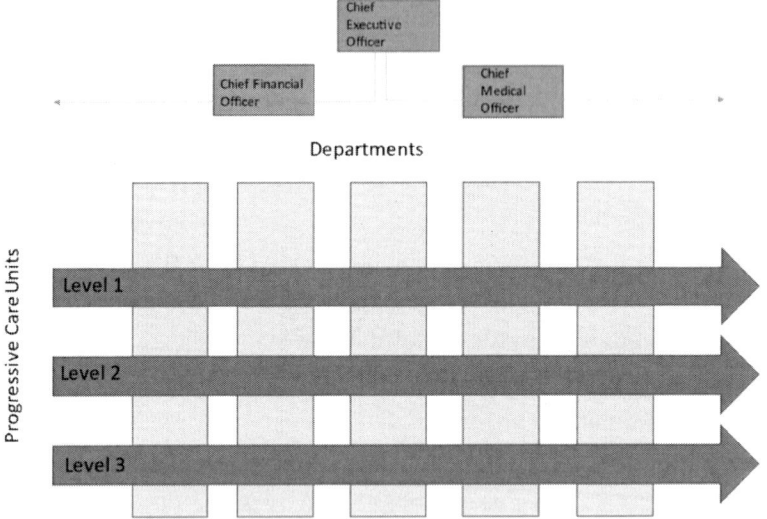

Source: Author's elaboration.

Figure 2. The progressive patient care organizational model.

As mentioned, the concrete drivers to assign patients to hospital units are based on two criteria. The first refers to their expected length-of-stay. Wards such as day-surgery/day-hospital, short-stay hospital, week hospital (for patients admitted on Mondays/Tuesdays and discharged within Saturdays), long stay-low care all belong to this criterion. The second has to do with patients' needs in terms of level of nursing assistance required or degree of dependency on medical equipment. For example, in Great Britain a new classification has been proposed based on four levels of patient dependency (O'Dea, Pepperman, and Bion 2003):

- level 0, patients receiving normal in-patient care with no special requirements;

- level 1, patients requiring additional monitoring and support above that which can be provided safely in an ordinary ward;
- level 2, patients requiring single organ system support excluding mechanical ventilation;
- level 3, patients requiring multiple organ system support or mechanical ventilation.

Finally, this organizational model often holds on separate pathways and flows for inpatients and outpatients, as well as for the emergency cases which no longer interfere with scheduled patients' admissions and treatment. Figure 2 provides a graphical representation of the progressive patient care model.

2.4. THE PATIENT-CENTERED APPROACH

In time, hospitals have further switched to new organizational solutions in response to the challenges they face and to the emerging role they cover within the network of actors in the healthcare system. As mentioned, the focus has gradually shifted from a hospital- or setting-centric approach to a patient-centered approach, meaning that each setting should be thought of as part of the network of actors involved in patients' continuum of care. In specific reference to hospitals, this means that their design and managerial approach must evolve according to this new focus on the centrality of patients.

The "patient-centered" approach has inspired new organizational models, characterized by flattened hierarchies and empowered horizontal organizational platforms. The latter are frequently led by new professional figures and populated by multi-professional teams. The run towards efficiency has also been implemented with techniques aimed at making processes flow smoothly and efficiently.

The patient-centered model is strictly connected to the progressive patient care organizational model and further emphasizes its horizontal reconfiguration. The model is built around transversal clinical pathways, in which patients are grouped based on their main pathology. In particular, the focus must now be placed on these pathways and on the set of processes that support them. These include all core clinical processes (medical visits, medical exams, etc.), as well as non-core processes, which do not determine the status of health directly, but are indeed fundamental for the primary clinical process (Villa 2012). These include processes such as, for example, pharmaceutical logistics, patient transportation or laboratory and imaging activities. In other words, this approach aims at reshaping hospital care delivery processes around the needs of patients and away from the traditional physicians-centered view (Buchan, Hancock, and Rafferty 1997; Coulson-Thomas 1997; Plsek 1997), in such a way that all (human, technological, etc.) resources merge into the pathway when needed by the patient (Rathert, Wyrwich, and Boren 2012). This must of course be done across all the settings the patient is likely to cross (e.g., emergency departments, operating rooms, intensive care units, wards, post-acute care settings). Numerous studies show that some of the major problems hospitals face often depend on a poor management of patient flows. This can lead to clinical mistakes, queues and delays, under- and over-capacity utilization, patient acceptance in inappropriate settings, variability of workload and stress for hospital staff (for example, Haraden and Resar 2004; Litvak et al. 2008). As a matter of fact, many authors suggest that hospitals should be viewed as complex systems made up of several internal sub-components that are tightly interdependent with each other (Litvak et al. 2008; Zonderland et al. 2010). To pursue quality and efficiency, therefore, it is fundamental to address the overall cycle of care globally, from the patient's first access to his/her discharge and follow-up, and not merely bits and pieces of the pathway, addressed disjointly. This brings us back to the progressive patient pooling approach, since a relevant aspect outlined by many studies is that patient flow problems are likely to occur when hospital resources (beds, operating rooms, human resources, etc.) are allocated in rigid ways and not regularly reallocated based on actual patients' needs (Walley and Steyn 2006). Figure 3 provides a graphical representation of the patient-centered organizational model.

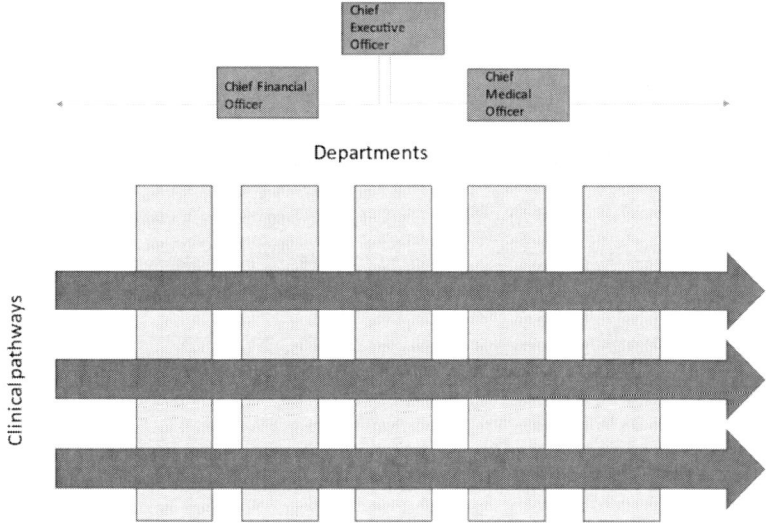

Source: Author's elaboration.

Figure 3. The patient-centered organizational model.

2.5. EMERGING HOSPITAL ORGANIZATIONAL CHARTS

It is important to clarify that organizational models are not necessarily alternative to each other and that, on the contrary, change frequently occurs incrementally. The clinical directorate model presents undoubted advantages in fostering specialized clinical competencies as well as in delegating responsibilities to lower hierarchical levels. A very centralized approach, on the contrary, is quite unlikely to be successful in hospitals. This is because of their complexity, with uncountable decisions taken every day and the inevitable risk of slowing down processes if these must necessarily be taken at the central level. Moreover, professionals (at all levels of the hierarchy) are usually highly educated and are unlikely to receive strict directives from top managers in a favorable way (King et al. 2015). Quite on the contrary, they often dispose of information and competencies that are not present in top hierarchical levels and must therefore necessarily enjoy a high degree of autonomy in conducting their own activities. The clinical directorate model, therefore, highly supports this trend of decentralization.

Therefore, rather than thinking of the progressive patient care and the patient-centered models as organizational solutions that overcome the clinical directorate one, it is maybe more reasonable to think of them as forms of *integration* of it. This interpretation is probably more realistic and can be confirmed in the typical organizational charts hospitals adopt in developed countries. These are typically matrices, in which traditional vertical responsibility units (clinical directorates) co-exist with more recent horizontal/transversal ones. These may be related to progressive intensity of care units or to clinical pathways built around a pathology (or both). While in the first case it is possibly more frequent for these organizational units to be directly assigned with relevant financial and non-financial resources, this is less frequently the case with clinical pathways. Although they are quickly gaining organizational relevance in many areas of the world, these still often appear as rather unstructured and less autonomous if compared to vertical units (Lega and De Pietro 2005). It may indeed be the case that they are not even clearly formalized within the organizational chart, and if they are, it is quite rare that their role and degree of autonomy are comparable to that of clinical directorates. Nevertheless, specific organizational equilibria may vary considerably across hospitals, and some may have already invested in a strong transition towards horizontal models. Great variability exists on the extent to which resources and autonomy are balanced between vertical and horizontal settings. Independently from the specific features of hospitals, however, international organizational trends are shifting towards mixed models in which the horizontal dimension(s) is (are) increasing in relevance, so as to face the main challenges of our times. Figure 4 represents a typical matrix configuration of hospital organizational charts.

The rest of this book is dedicated to exploring the articulated set of decisions top management is called to make while driving organizational change towards hospital performance, in coherence with these trends of transformation. It explores the set of tools it has at its disposal to implement new organizational models successfully, so as to translate hospitals' strategy into practice.

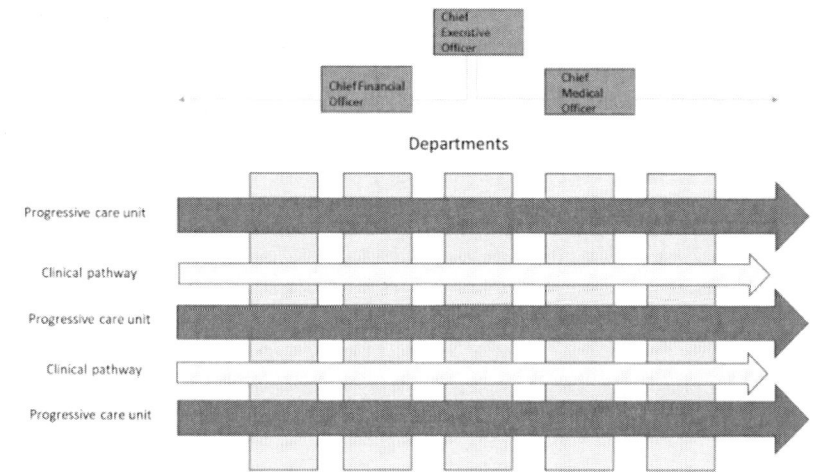

Source: Author's elaboration

Figure 4. A matrix configuration of a hospital's organizational chart.

CONCLUSION

Hospital organizational models are at the basis of the uncountable processes and praxes that make up hospital activity. They are the consequence of hospitals' strategies and affect them deeply in the long run. This is in part due to the difficulty of changing them, given that transforming an organizational chart requires massive managerial effort in practically every corner of the hospital. Nevertheless, in coherence with the main pressures coming from the context in which they operate, hospitals are indeed called to update their organizational charts. If they don't, they will inevitably incur into situations in which their organizational assets do not support the activities they are required to carry out.

Although hospitals may differ across countries, regions, or even within the same city, many of their characterizing features are surprisingly similar. This is because the challenges they face and the pressures they must respond to are global and require similar solutions. Therefore, although organizational charts may differ to some extent from hospital to hospital and may be adapted to specific contexts, the main trends described in this chapter are likely to be relevant worldwide.

REFERENCES

Andrews, R., Beynon, M. J., and McDermott, A. 2019. "Configurations of New Public Management Reforms and the Efficiency, Effectiveness and Equity of Public Healthcare Systems: A Fuzzy-Set Qualitative Comparative Analysis." *Public Management Review* 21 (8): 1236–60. https://doi.org/10.1080/14719037.2018.1561927.

Bokhour, B. G., Fix, G. M., Mueller, N. M., Barker, A. M., LaVela, S. L., Hill, J. N., Solomon, J. L., and C. Vandeusen Luka, C. 2018. "How Can Healthcare Organizations Implement Patient-Centered Care? Examining a Large-Scale Cultural Transformation How Can Healthcare Organizations Implement Patient-Centered Care? Examining a Large-Scale Cultural Transformation BFix GMueller N et al. See More Health Services Research, (2018), 18(1)." *BMC Health Services Research* 18 (1): 1–11.

Braithwaite, J., Westbrook, M. T., Hindle, D., Iedema, R. A., and Black, D. A. 2006. "Does Restructuring Hospitals Results in Greater Efficiency? - An Empirical Test Using Diachronic Data." *Health Services Management Research* 19 (1): 1–12. https://doi.org/10.1258/095148406775322016.

Braithwaite, J., Westbrook, M. T., Iedema, R., Mallock, N. A., Forsyth, R., and Zhang, K. 2005. "A Tale of Two Hospitals: Assessing Cultural Landscapes and Compositions." *Social Science and Medicine* 60 (5): 1149–62. https://doi.org/10.1016/j.socscimed.2004.06.046.

Buchan, J., Hancock, C., and Rafferty, A. 1997. "Health Sector Reform and Trends in the United Kingdom Hospital Workforce." *Med Care.* 35 (10): 135–50.

Caffrey, L., Ferlie, E., and McKevitt, C. 2019. "The Strange Resilience of New Public Management: The Case of Medical Research in the UK's National Health Service." *Public Management Review* 21 (4): 537–58. https://doi.org/10.1080/14719037.2018.1503702.

Colamesta, V., Dugo, V., La Milia, D., Sommella, L., Orsi, G., Bucci, R., De Vito, C., et al. 2018. "Intermediate Care Units in Progressive Patient Care Model: A Systematic Literature Review." *Epidemiology Biostatistics and Public Health*, no. 4.

Correia, T., and Denis, J. L. 2016. "Hybrid Management, Organizational Configuration, and Medical Professionalism: Evidence from the Establishment of a Clinical Directorate in Portugal." *BMC Health Services Research* 16 (2). https://doi.org/10.1186/s12913-016-1398-2.

Coulson-Thomas, C. 1997. "Re-Engineering Hospital and Healthcare Processes." *Health Estate J.* 51 (7): 14–15.

Gabutti, I., Mascia, D., and Cicchetti, A. 2017. "Exploring 'Patient-Centered' Hospitals: A Systematic Review to Understand Change." *BMC Health Services Research* 17 (1). https://doi.org/10.1186/s12913-017-2306-0.

Gabutti, I., and Morandi, F. 2018. "HRM Practices and Organizational Change: Evidence from Italian Clinical Directorates." *Health Services Management Research*. https://doi.org/10.1177/0951484818790213.

Gabutti, I., and Cicchetti, A. 2017. "Translating Strategy into Practice: A Tool to Understand Organizational Change in a Spanish University Hospital. An in-Depth Analysis in Hospital Clinic." *International Journal of Healthcare Management* 13 (2): 142–55. https://doi.org/10.1080/20479700.2017.1336837.

Haraden, C., and Resar, R. 2004. "Patient Flow in Hospitals: Understanding and Controlling It Better." *Frontiers of Health Services Management* 20 (4): 3–15.

King, O., Nancarrow, S. A., Borthwick, A. M., and Grace, S. 2015. "Contested Professional Role Boundaries in Health Care: A Systematic Review of the Literature." *Journal of Foot and Ankle Research* 8 (1): 1–9. https://doi.org/10.1186/s13047-015-0061-1.

Lega, F., and De Pietro, C. 2005. "Converging Patterns in Hospital Organization: Beyond the Professional Bureaucracy." *Health Policy* 74.

Lega, F. 2007. "Organisational Design for Health Integrated Delivery Systems: Theory and Practice." *Health Policy* 81: 258–79.

Lega, F. 2008. "The Rise and Fall(Acy) of Clinical Directorates in Italy." *Health Policy* 85 (2): 252–62. https://doi.org/10.1016/j.healthpol.2007.07.010.

Litvak, N., Van Rijsbergen, M., Boucherie, R., and Van Houdenhoven, M. 2008. "Managing the Overflow of Intensive Care Patients." *Eur J Oper Res* 185 (3): 998–1010.

Mascia, D., Morandi, F., and Cicchetti, A. 2014. "Looking Good or Doing Better? Patterns of Decoupling in the Implementation of Clinical Directorates." *Health Care Management Review* 39 (2): 111–23. https://doi.org/10.1097/HMR.0b013e318286095c.

Mei, J., and Kirkpatrick, I. 2019. "Public Hospital Reforms in China: Towards a Model of New Public Management?" *International Journal of Public Sector Management* 32 (4): 352–66. https://doi.org/10.1108/IJPSM-03-2018-0063.

Mintzberg, H.. 1997. "Toward Healthier Hospitals." *Health Care Manage Rev.* 22: 9–18.

Moresi-Izzo, S., Bankauskaite, V., and Gericke, C.A. 2010. "The Effect of Market Reforms and New Public Management Mechanisms on the Swiss Health Care System." *International Journal of Health Planning and Management* 25 (4): 368–85. https://doi.org/10.1002/hpm.1026.

Norrish, B., and Rundall, T. 2001. "Hospital Restructuring and the Work of Registered Nurses." *Milbank Q.* 79 (1): 55–79.

O'Dea, J., Pepperman, M., and Bion, J. 2003. "Comprehensive Critical Care: A National Strategic Framework in All but Name." *Intensive Care Med.*

Plsek, P. 1997. "Systematic Design of Healthcare Processes." *Qual Health Care* 6 (1): 40.

Rathert, C., Wyrwich, M., and Boren, S. 2012. "Patient-Centered Care and Outcomes: A Systematic Review of the Literature." *Med Care Res Rev.* 70 (4): 351–79.

Simonet, D. 2014. "Assessment of New Public Management in Health Care: The French Case." *Health and Quality of Life Outcomes* 12 (1): 1–9. https://doi.org/10.1186/1478-4505-12-57_old.

Villa, S., Barbieri, M., and Lega F. 2009. "Restructuring Patient Flow Logistics around Patient Care Needs: Implications and Practicalities from Three Critical Cases." *Health Care Manag Sci.*, 155–65.

Villa, S. 2012. "Operations Management a Support Del Sistema Di Operazioni Aziendali. Modelli Di Analisi e Soluzioni Progettuali per Il Settore Sanitario." *CEDAM*. ["Operations Management to Support the Business Operations System. Analysis Models and Design Solutions for the Healthcare Sector."]

Walley, P., and Steyn, R. 2006. "Managing Variation in Demand: Lessons Fromthe UK National Health Service." *J Healthc Manag* 51 (5): 309–20.

Zonderland, M. E., Boucherie, R. J., Litvak, N., and Vleggeert-Lankamp, C. L. A. M. 2010. "Planning and Scheduling of Semi-Urgent Surgeries." *Health Care Management Science* 13 (3): 256–67. https://doi.org/10.1007/s10729-010-9127-6.

Chapter 3

MANAGING A HOSPITAL IS LIKE CONDUCTING AN ORCHESTRA

ABSTRACT

Multiple managerial tools are key in driving change in hospitals successfully. These include managerial accounting (MA) tools, health technology management (HTM) tools, information communication technology (ICT) tools, human resource management (HRM) tools.

MA tools must be re-designed based on new organizational charts. The set of indicators to assess hospital performance must be related to the accomplishments of multi-professional teams working across units' (and organizational) boundaries. HTM tools must make use of Health Technology Assessment to adopt, implement, and dismiss costly technologies in optimal ways. There exist different contextual organizational factors that are likely to affect technologies' success. These must be taken into account when performing such assessments. The ICT system must be designed around the hospital's organizational model. Communication must be built around clinical pathways (and not around static organizational settings) to guarantee smooth patient flows within and outside the hospital. HRM must be coherent with the hospital's configuration. Professional roles must be updated. Competencies must be mapped, developed, and monitored to assure an effective functioning of organizational units. Career pathways must be updated to encourage the assumption of responsibility in horizontal settings.

Keywords: managerial accounting tools, health technology management tools, information communication technology tools, human resource management tools.

3.1. INTRODUCTION

Implementing new organizational solutions implies driving numerous managerial interventions coherently. Each one of these must be effective in the short run but must also support the overall success of the hospital's strategy in the long one. Managerial accounting tools, health technology management tools, information communication technology tools, human resource management tools are all managerial tools that must ultimately be used in coherence with the hospital's organizational chart. Any systematic deviation in how these are built and implemented from the organization's strategy, is likely to cause discrepancies between the model that is formally adopted and the one that is (naturally) implemented. This phenomenon, named decoupling, is likely to have deleterious effects on hospitals and on healthcare systems in general.

3.2. THE MAIN DIMENSIONS OF HOSPITAL MANAGEMENT

Leading and managing hospitals requires unique, yet very heterogeneous competencies and attitudes. The intrinsic complexity of hospitals implies a strong ability in driving all its features towards common goals simultaneously. Not only are hospitals characterized by many organizational units, but each of these carries out numerous and different processes. Each of these must somehow be reconducted to a common framework if the hospital is to achieve its strategic objectives.

In other words, it is very difficult to translate strategy into practice because of the uncountable dynamics that are potentially able to interfere with its concrete implementation. Moreover, hospitals' stakeholders and the professionals who work in them are so heterogeneous that even just *convincing* them to adapt to a common strategy is challenging. Managing a hospital is like conducting an orchestra: each instrument must be played at the right place, in the right moment and in the right way. Even just a minor mistake or inaccuracy will make the symphony just not sound right. If this happens, the scrupulous work of the rest of the orchestra risks being ruined. Out of metaphor, hospital management must design an appropriate organizational model and implement it by using the various managerial tools at its disposal. Although they are numerous, they must be driven in coherent ways and must all be consistent with the hospital's main strategies. Although this may appear obvious in principle, the complexity of hospitals easily leads to misalignments and contradictions in the use of this set of tools.

Furthermore, each component of this managerial intervention must be assessed in a timely way. Each must be therefore linked to its relevant potential outputs and dimensions of performance. Performance (in its complex acceptation which is described in Chapter 4) must be monitored systematically and pro-actively. Any discrepancy from the expected strategic results must necessarily be detected promptly and the right managerial interventions must be introduced to cover such gaps quickly. Indeed, if these gaps are not detected and corrected on time, the risk is to incur decoupling phenomena (Lega, Longo, and Rotolo 2013; Holt et al. 2018). These consist in the adoption and the contextual non-implementation of organizational models, practices, or rules that are only formally adopted by the organization (Ruef and Scott 1998; Scott and Ruef 2000). The danger of decoupling phenomena lies in the inability of the organization in reaching its strategic goals and, in general, the risk of losing control over the concrete dynamics that get rooted within its boundaries. Therefore, delays in detecting such trends may be extremely dangerous and costly, given the strong difficulty of "correcting" undesired praxes and dynamics in highly complex contexts.

More specifically, hospital managers must use the following tools to drive the hospital towards its "perfect symphony". First, it must structure and implement an effective managerial accounting system. This is the first fundamental step because if any problem or inconsistency occurs and this is not detected quickly, its consequences are likely to affect many settings, processes, and activities in drastic ways (Keel et al. 2020). Second, it must adopt, implement, and dismiss health technologies effectively. Health technologies are usually extremely expensive and may bind hospitals financially for years or even decades. Moreover, their impact on the quality of hospital services is very relevant, implying that if not managed in a fully aware manner, professionals may not be put in the position of performing independently from their competencies and efforts (Grossi et al. 2019). Third, managers must guarantee effective, timely, safe, and exhaustive information flows. They must ensure an easy access to relevant information to all the professionals who need them to carry out their duties. Implementing a well-structured information communication system is even more arduous given the "scattered scenarios" in which health services are usually provided. Although hospitals may be physically located in one or in few buildings, their activities are highly interconnected with those of other providers of care and stakeholders. This implies that communication and information must flow smoothly also outside the hospital's boundaries (Gray et al. 2018). Fourth, managers must drive human resources towards the hospital's common objectives. This is challenging given the heterogeneity of hospital professionals (e.g., physicians, nurses, other clinical professionals, biologists, economists, legal professionals) and given the high autonomy they usually enjoy. These professionals are usually highly educated and may tend to resist to coercive managerial approaches based on top-town directives (Trebble et al. 2014).

In conclusion, it is worth mentioning that these features must all be managed in a highly institutionalized context, with very high pressures coming from the external (but also internal) environment (Gabutti 2019). Failing in managing even only one aspect of these intertwining dimensions, would inevitably lead to decoupling phenomena and to a tangled set of uncontrollable dynamics able to hinder top level hospital results.

3.3. MANAGERIAL ACCOUNTING TOOLS

3.3.1. Understanding the Managerial Accounting System of a Hospital

Healthcare organizations have, by now, grown confident in the adoption of evolved managerial accounting tools (Gao and Gurd 2015; Keel et al. 2020; Krupička 2021). As is the case with all the other features of hospital management, it is key that these develop in harmony with organizational trends. Furthermore, these tools should not be intended as mere technical tools aimed at controlling a long list of performance indicators. Rather, they may be thought of as strategic tools capable of directing the behaviors of professionals towards (or away from) the organization's main goals. These tools can therefore offer strong support to the implementation of strategic change, but, on the other hand, may lead to insurmountable obstacles to the achievement of strategic objectives if not used adequately.

Managing a hospital implies three levels of analysis:

- strategic planning (decisions on strategic objectives),
- directional control (decisions on *how* to reach strategic objectives, through which actions),
- operative control (monitoring the enhancement of specific behaviors and actions).

The managerial accounting system (and the budgeting system in particular) belongs to the second level. Nevertheless, it is strictly connected to the other two and should never be managed in isolation from them. In the first place it must purse the objectives of strategic planning (level 1), in which management assesses different strategic options and selects the best. This is done after careful analysis of the opportunities and threats coming from the environment. Second, it sets the bases for a structured and routinized operative control (level 3), in which actions and behaviors are assessed regularly and ultimately reconducted to the priorities set in the managerial accounting system itself.

Specifically, the managerial accounting system must formally and explicitly correlate three dimensions: the hospital's organizational structure, the main objectives to be pursued in the short/mid-term, the resources available. This occurs through the budgeting process which defines short-term objectives as well as the available range of time to reach them. Resources, therefore, are assigned to organizational units accordingly and performance measurement systems are defined. Figure 5 provides a representation of the relationship between a hospital's managerial accounting system and the other dimensions mentioned.

Designing, implementing, and updating a managerial accounting system in a complex organization can, however, be very challenging (Douglas et al. 2019). Different forms of coherence must be pursued and monitored simultaneously. Strategic, organizational, behavioral, managerial, and temporal coherence must all be sought to guarantee a solid and well-structured measurement system. In Table 1 these main forms of coherence are briefly described and related to a hospital's managerial accounting system.

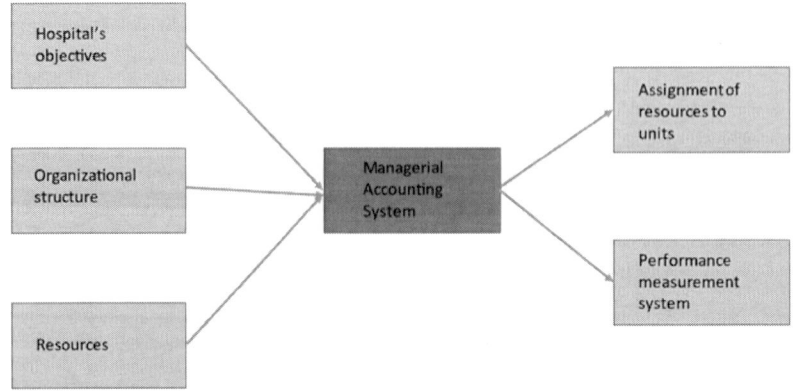

Source: Author's re-elaboration from Sacco 2019.

Figure 5. The role of the managerial accounting system within a hospital.

Table 1. The different levels of coherence of managerial accounting systems within hospitals

Level of coherence	Brief description	Examples of questions to be answered
Strategic	Coherence with external-environmental factors, internal factors, temporal planning	Is the MA system coherent with the laws and social priorities in the environment? Is the MA system coherent with the staffing and technological equipment available in the hospital? Is the MA system coherent with both long-term and short-term objectives?
Organizational	Coherence with the hospital's vertical and horizontal dimensions	Does there exist coherence in the cascading of objectives from central to unit level? (vertical coherence) Are objectives distributed in a just and logical way across units on the same hierarchical level? (horizontal coherence)
Behavioral	Coherence between performance evaluation at the organizational and individual levels	Are organizational objectives translated into individual or team-objectives in an effective way? Does there exist a reasonable balance between the hospital's need of controlling individuals and of fostering their autonomy and commitment?
Managerial	Coherence between MA system and main managerial priorities	Is the MA system coherent with managerial directives in terms of transparency and anti-corruption? Is the MA system coherent with the development strategies of human resources in different units?
Temporal	Coherence of objectives in time	Are the objectives assigned realistic and coherent with previous results and trends? Are budgeting systems coherent with reporting ones?

Source: Author's elaboration.

Pursuing these forms of coherence implies diminishing the risk of incurring loosely coupled organizations. In these, organizational units are not effectively inter-connected and each tends to pursue its own specific objectives, failing in prioritizing general organizational ones. If this happens, individual organizational units or functions do not clearly commit to their specific role within the wider organization. In this way they tend to operate as isolated monads, diverting efforts from the attainment of central strategies. Moreover, gaps between formal directives or rules and concrete behaviors, is typical of loosely coupled organizations. Formal rules may be adopted to obtain legitimation from the external environment, but a lack of overall coherence in the managerial accounting system may encourage decoupling phenomena and eradicate routines that deviate from the intended behaviors. More in general, this can lead to discrepancies between decisions at the central level and at the professional/individual level, causing conflict and ambiguity within the hospital.

Goal ambiguity must be firmly countered by the managerial accounting system due to its frequently devastating effects on overall performance (Calciolari, Cantu, and Fattore 2011). Goal ambiguity may take the form of an ambiguity in the actual understanding of the mission of a function or unit. For example, whether the human resource management function should be intended as a function responsible for administrative matters only or rather as a strategic partner of the upper echelon of the organization, may vary considerably across organizations. Managerial accounting systems are co-responsible in clearly defining this role. Furthermore, goal ambiguity may concern means vs. ends, meaning that it may not always be clear whether an action is a means to obtain something else or rather an end itself. Managerial accounting systems that fail in clarifying these aspects may lead to frustration in pursuing objectives that are not contextualized within a broader achievement. Priority ambiguity is a further form of goal ambiguity. Complex organizations hold on multiple dimensions of performance (Carini et al. 2020). These may at times appear in contrast and specific professions, units or even individuals may have different perceptions of the priorities they should pursue. An effective managerial accounting system must connect, balance, and complement such dimensions within units and within the hospital in general. Finally, target and timeline ambiguity may constitute forms of goal ambiguity too. Developing a clear understanding of the specific targets expected by professionals as well as in which timing, are key objectives of managerial accounting systems if they are to enhance behaviors that are concretely oriented towards strategic objectives.

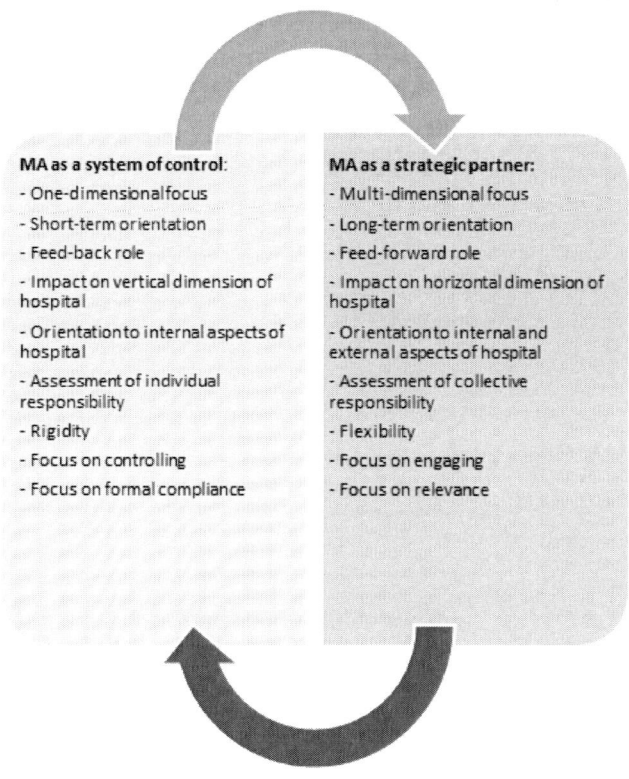

Source: Author's re-elaboration from Sacco 2019.

Figure 6. Managerial accounting intended as a controlling vs. strategic tool.

Indeed, managerial accounting systems may be thought of as a set of monitoring tools aimed at shaping and guiding individual behaviors towards common goals, rather than mere and complex measurement systems that trace specific actions or behaviors analytically. An excessively high degree of specificity in a highly complex organization, such as a hospital, may lead to an unrestrained degree of formalization which, in turn, may hinder flexibility, resilience, and the hospital's actual ability of changing, according both to external pressures as well as to its own strategies.

The difficulty of implementing effective managerial accounting systems in hospitals is not only tied to the goal of pursuing overall coherence. Their actual role in hospitals may be interpreted in different ways and, in fact, the more hospitals evolve towards articulated organizational solutions, the more frequently managerial accounting is called to evolve from a mere control system to that of a strategic support to top management, coherently with what stated above. This implies dealing simultaneously with operative control-oriented but also strategic-oriented perspectives. The main differences these two perspectives imply are summarized in Figure 6.

3.3.2. Strategic Solutions in the Design of the Managerial Accounting System of a Hospital

The gradual shift of managerial accounting systems towards a strategic role in support of top management, has fostered the need to allow managers to "see" organizational performance under different perspectives simultaneously. These can be split into three families: items that enable hospital activities; activities themselves; outcomes. In this sense, managerial accounting systems should be designed in such a way as to provide a clear picture of "how well" the hospital is doing in each of these three dimensions. Indeed, if the hospital is not in possess of the necessary enabling items, it will not be able to implement its intended activities and achieve intended outcomes. If it is weak in implementing its activities, although it may be in possess of the required tools to do so, it is still likely to fail in achieving its intended outcomes. Or also, if it is successful in providing enabling items and implementing activities but still, for some reason, does not reach its expected outcomes, its final performance is of course disappointing. Adopting this sort of "strategic map" allows management to detect the most problematic managerial areas in the organization and to plan targeted interventions directly addressed to the weak links of the chain. Figure 7 provides a representation of how hospital objectives may be reconducted to these three families.

Adopting strategic maps provides hospital management with a multi-dimensional perspective on how the hospital is performing. This is key in determining the priorities to be implemented in a selective way. This also guides managers in linking logically cause and effects, enabling them to achieve desirable results. Finally, these maps are fundamental in assigning responsibilities and contributions to the achievement of organizational strategies in a clear way.

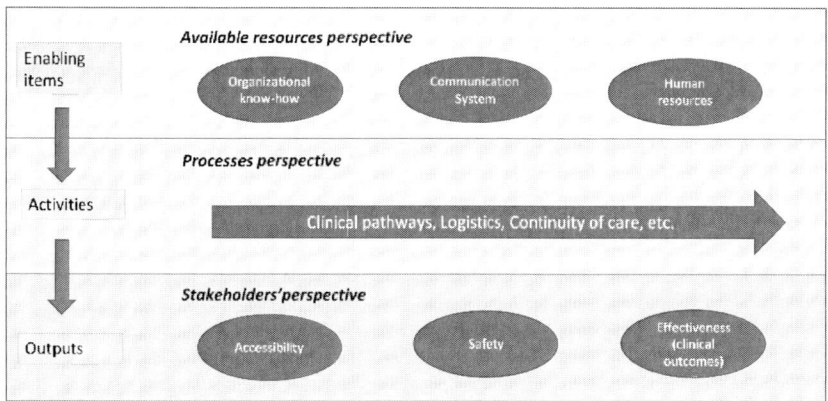

Source: Author's re-elaboration from Sacco 2019.

Figure 7. The various perspectives of managerial accounting systems within hospitals and some examples of each.

This multi-dimensional approach is by now fundamental to overcome some major limits of traditional mono-dimensional managerial accounting systems, which would inevitably lead to numerous but fragmented measuring initiatives. This new approach allows to deal effectively with the following issues:

- balancing cost-containment in the short-term with expensive investments that can enhance benefits in the long one;

- defining a clear and nitid value proposition for patients and for other stakeholders (e.g., institutions, the broader community);
- assessing clearly the hospital's ability of implementing key processes efficiently and coherently (hence producing value through them);
- leading the hospital towards an effective innovation plan which is coherent with its overall strategy;
- enhancing a concrete *organizational readiness to change*, which implies that all innovative initiatives are clearly related to and coherent with the hospital's objectives.

Indeed, traditional managerial accounting approaches have often failed in detecting many key issues in support of the organizational strategy. First, they frequently do not detect a vast array of phenomena that are not strictly related to accounting matters. They are rarely able to provide a concrete understanding of the implementation of processes and, even more importantly, of the contribution of the hospital to dynamics that are also external to its boundaries. They frequently fail in detecting the performance of teams, especially in those (frequent) cases in which teams do not necessarily coincide with organizational units. In general, they are unable to "go beyond" the mere observation of an isolated phenomenon and to connect the multitude of phenomena within the organizational context. This means incurring a standard and reiterated managerial accounting system that does not evolve coherently with the development of new strategies. Implementing an integrated and dynamic managerial accounting approach, which is truly able to link actions and effects and to share this knowledge across all levels of the hospital, is by now a clear priority in most hospitals.

A key and revolutionary aspect of "modern" managerial accounting systems is indeed the fact that they should be built around transversal processes (Vina et al. 2009). This is the way to foster true integration within the hospital. Hospital processes are uncountable and very different in nature. They may range from logistics related to the use of medical devices, to the implementation of clinical procedures, to – in the most extended sense of the term – clinical pathways, which sequentially define the typical steps patients follow during their stay within the hospital (as well as outside its boundaries). If managerial accounting is truly successful in assessing processes, hospitals can overcome the traditional fragmented perspective which so frequently leads to taking arbitrary decisions, without fully understanding their full effects. An integrated system, moreover, will help hospitals to reduce duplications, redundancies and all sorts of activities that are not producing added value within overall processes (Ling et al. 2010; Cash-Gibson et al. 2019).

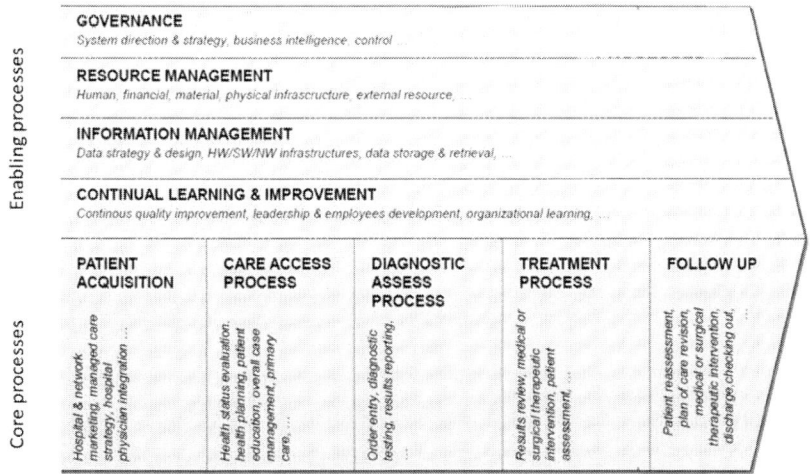

Source: Author's re-elaboration from Sacco 2019.

Figure 8. A representation of key processes within hospitals.

Thinking in terms of processes and centering measurement systems on their implementation constitutes a deep change towards an approach that can potentially affect every part of the hospital. Processes are indeed everywhere and at the basis of everything that is done within hospitals. These may be of support (enabling processes) or may be core processes that are directly responsible for the hospital's outcomes (Kriegel et al. 2019). For example, many human resource management or information communication activities may be considered support processes. Clinical pathways, on the other hand, can be thought of as hospital core processes.

If they switch from a unit or setting-oriented perspective to a process-oriented one, managerial accounting systems can detect in transparency those items that are able to cause a hospital's final outcome: the health of its patients. Figure 8 shows some of the main enabling and core processes in hospitals.

How can this transition be carried out concretely? It is well known that implementing change in a complex organization frequently requires incremental forms of change (Ileri and Arik 2018). The resistances that may emerge towards "new ways of working" as well as the extrinsic complexity in changing managerial approaches that affect many different issues simultaneously, suggest that radical forms of change may be too risky and likely to fail. Possibly, the same holds true when transforming managerial accounting systems in hospitals (Mannion and Braithwaite 2012). It is not easy to change what is measured, how it is measured, by whom it is measured and how these measurements are then used without incurring extended discontent. Moreover, the large dimensions and complexity of hospitals imply that managerial accounting should indeed be designed *also* around physical units and traditional responsibility centers. If organizational charts are still based on vertical responsibility units which are accountable for the resources that are assigned to them, these must necessarily be monitored through an adequate managerial accounting system. Therefore, we can think of incremental and gradual managerial accounting transition plans, which gradually shift from approaches that are merely based on vertical units to mixed ones. These, as mentioned, should integrate traditional ones by introducing an approach based on hospital processes, in the perspective of a matrix scheme. In Figure 9 a graphical representation of a transition plan from a traditional to an "evolved" managerial accounting system is provided.

Implementing integrated managerial accounting systems implies integration among processes and phases, among functions and units, among different professionals. Moreover, if the hospital is indeed intended as an actor within a broader network, integration should really be among different organizations, so as to detect and evaluate their joint contribution to the final creation of value.

Managing a Hospital is Like Conducting an Orchestra 47

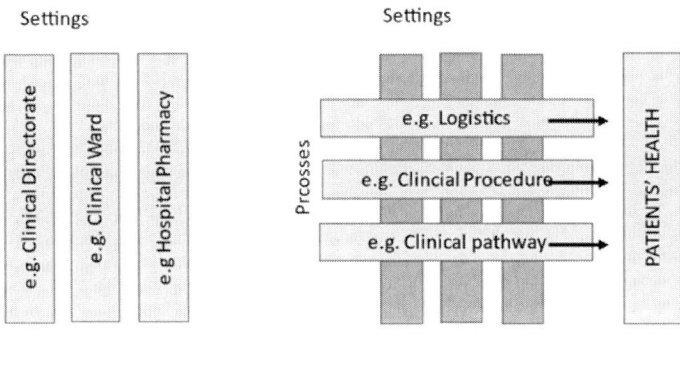

Source: Author's elaboration.

Figure 9. A gradual transition from a setting-oriented managerial accounting system to an integrated one.

Integration is the logic at the basis of approaches such as activity-based costing (in support of activity-based management) (Cardinaels, Roodhooft, and Van Herck 2004; Ortaköylü et al. 2016; Keel et al. 2017). The idea is to link costs no longer to organizational units on the mere basis of the organizational chart, but rather to refer them to those activities that are directly responsible for the achievement of final outputs. Activity based costing can link resources to outcomes directly and can detect more or less effective ways of consuming the former. This approach is considered by many an innovative and promising way of structuring managerial accounting systems in healthcare due to several reasons. First, hospitals' responsibility centers involved in the processes of care are increasing in number and in type, challenging therefore traditional systems based on traditional responsibility centers. Second, indirect costs are typically increasing, generating the need of developing new and accurate ways of assigning them to such centers of responsibility. Finally, the conception of health services provided in transversal clinical pathways and, in general, the new highly process-oriented culture of hospitals, imply the capability of measuring items across the rigid boundaries of organizational units. Figure 10 shows a conceptual representation of activity-based costing.

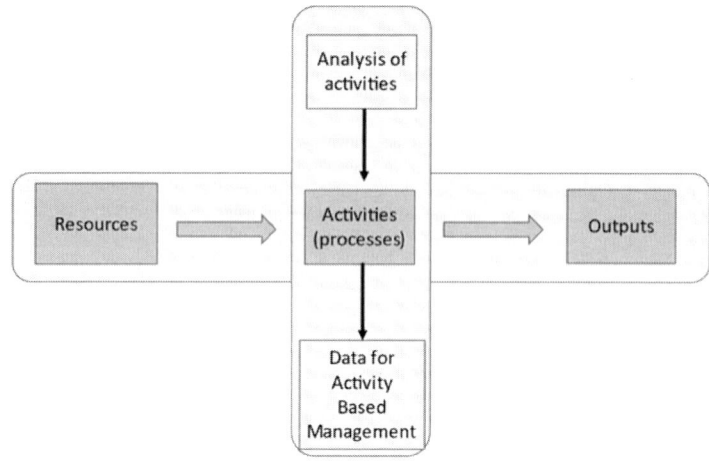

Source: Author's elaboration.

Figure 10. A conceptual representation of activity-based costing.

Such an approach when measuring costs implies a structured methodology to understand the real costs behind different components of hospital activity. This fosters a deeper awareness in the assessment of different alternatives in the creation of value. Adopting this approach is, however, undoubtedly complicated and challenging. It is costly and difficult to implement in settings that are possibly characterized by consolidated praxes, such as hospitals. Its introduction, therefore, is likely to be successful only through gradual steps. These should preserve an orientation towards an accountability of "traditional" units, while introducing parallel or complementary objectives referred to a joint responsibility across them. This transition may constitute a guiding process towards the shift from setting-centered to patient-centered hospitals.

3.4. HEALTH TECHNOLOGY MANAGEMENT TOOLS

A complex environment such as a hospital is affected deeply by the set of technologies within (or also outside) its boundaries. The term technology, in healthcare, may assume different meanings and its effective management implies a deep understanding of how different types of health technologies interact among each other and with the hospital's context in general.

Health technologies are "the application of organized knowledge and skills in the form of devices, medicines, vaccines, procedures and systems developed to solve a health problem and improve quality of lives" ("WHO/Europe|Health Technologies and Medicines - Health Technology Assessment" n.d.; Esmaeilzadeh et al. 2011). Their role in hospitals is key given their ability of affecting many aspects of the hospital's functioning and its overall performance. Health Technology Assessment is a multidimensional and multidisciplinary approach to assess the clinical, social, organizational, economic, ethical, and legal implications of the use of a health technology. Such assessment is based on the analysis of various dimensions such as, for example, safety, efficacy, costs, social and organizational impact. Health technology assessment assesses both the real and potential effects of technologies along their entire lifespan and constitutes a guiding principle for resource allocation both at organizational and policy levels.

Traditional health technology assessment carried out at national or regional levels has advanced considerably over the past years and has provided solid guidance in the effective adoption of health technologies. Technology adoption should reflect, for example, mandates, objectives, profiles of end-users. Moreover, health technology assessment not only concerns the mere adoption of technologies, but rather all the phases of technology management, including implementation and dismissal. The considerations concerning these phases, however, may need to be adapted at the hospital level. This is the level in which meso- and micro-decisions are taken. These concern, for example, the acquisition and use of a *specific* technology for a *specific* unit. Although health technology assessment, which is usually led at national or regional levels, is a highly valuable activity at hospital level too, its contribution to decision-making processes at the hospital level may be problematic, at times. This is why hospital-based health technology assessment has matured in the past years (Munn 2014; Halmesmäki, Pasternack, and Roine 2016), leading to debates on which guiding principles should be followed in its implementation. Hospital-based health technology assessment means performing health technology assessment activities tailored to the hospital context specifically, so as to drive managerial decisions and foster greater awareness on their effects. Table 2 displays a list of guiding principles for Hospital-based health technology assessment provided within the AdHopHTA research project ("AdHopHTA | A New European Project on Hospital Based Health Technology Assessment").

It is clear from these guiding principles that, to reach the extent of its potential, hospital-based health technology assessment should assume a strategic placement within hospitals. It should be conceived as a long-term investment with a clear role within the hospital. Its role should be envigored by the prestige and relevance of the professional positions it implies and should be nurtured in time through a continuous learning approach. Moreover, hospital-based health technology assessment should be intended as a highly participative process which involves all professionals concerned by the actual use of the technology. This participative feature reflects the necessity to design technology implementation strategies in a shared way, by recognizing needs and know-how of end users and of all the stakeholders affected by the technology in the first place. More in particular, in the light of the changing features of hospitals, this means that this participative approach should be tailored around the emerging organizational design and "ways of working" described in the previous sections of this book. If it is indeed the case that horizontal models imply a shared use of resources such as, in the first place, health technologies, such "bottom-up" participation should not be limited to specific traditional units, but rather extended to the multi-disciplinary teams that are likely to be affected by the technology.

Table 2. Guiding principles for Hospital-based health technology assessment

Dimensions	Guiding principles
1. The assessment process	1. The HB-HTA report should clearly state its goal and scope, reflect the hospital context, and take into account the informational needs of hospital decision makers. 2. The HB-HTA report should be performed systematically using good methods and appropriate tools in a way that can be adapted to other hospitals (transferable). 3. The HB-HTA process should involve all relevant stakeholders and be conducted in an unbiased and transparent manner ensuring independence and proper communication of its results to hospital stakeholders. 4. The mission, vision, and values of the HB-HTA unit should be clearly defined and coherent with the hospital's overall mission and strategy, and should allow for clear governance of the HB-HTA unit.
2. Leadership, strategy and partnerships	5. There should be clear leadership at the top of the HB-HTA unit as well as a communication policy/strategy. 6. Criteria for the selection of technologies to be assessed should be clearly stated. 7. Process of disinvestment of health technologies should be defined and established. 8. HB-HTA units should be willing to improve in the light of its experience and be open to learn and innovate. 9. There should be a clear policy and mechanisms for sharing knowledge and resources. 10. HB-HTA units should collaborate with regional, national, and international HTA organizations. 11. Links with key allies and partners should be proactively identified and promoted.
3. Resources	12. Well-defined human resources, recruitment policies, and career development plans should be established. 13. Financial resources should be sufficient to cover operational costs and ensure an appropriate place of work.
4. Impact	14. Short- and medium-term internal and external impact of the HB-HTA unit work should be measured. 15. Long-term impact of the HB-HTA unit on hospital performance and health of communities should be measured.

Source: ("AdHopHTA | A New European Project on Hospital Based Health Technology Assessment").

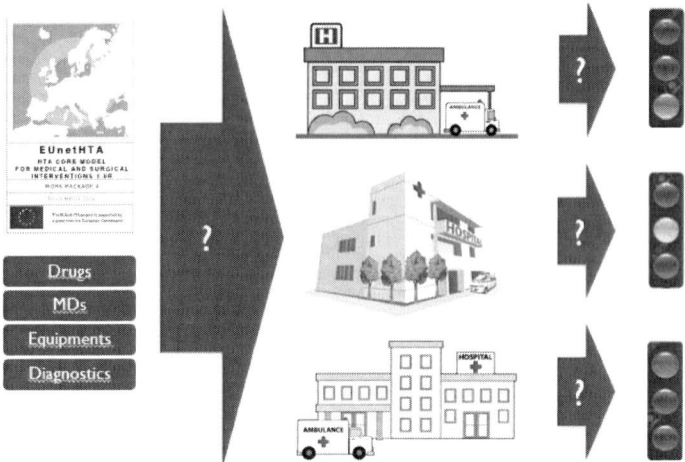

Source: Cicchetti 2019.

Figure 11. A representation of health technologies' variability in performance across different hospitals.

Failing in implementing these guiding principles may lead to relevant gaps between technologies' intended and concrete effects. Indeed, there persists a high variability in the concrete ability of hospitals in using health technologies (Grossi et al. 2019), even though they are assessed through national or regional health technology assessments. It is by now a common opinion that the production and diffusion of health technology assessment recommendations at national or regional levels alone, without an adequate contextualization in the specific hospital, do not automatically produce their intended effects in every organization (Kristensen, Nymann, and Konradsen 2016). Efforts in hospital-based health technology assessment as well as a deep analysis of hospitals' specific and relevant contextual characteristics, are key in pursuing effective management of technology. Failing in contextualizing evidence concerning any health technology may lead to unintended consequences in terms of hospital performance (Camberlin et al. 2021).

The relevance of hospitals' contextual characteristics on technology uptake has been partly disregarded in the past (Kringos et al. 2015). How they may affect technology adoption and, especially, implementation, has not always been explored clearly during hospital strategic decision-making. Indeed, most of the effort is usually focused on the process of formal adoption of technologies rather than on their concrete utilization and effective integration within (and outside) the organization (Gagnon et al. 2012; Kresswell and Sheikh 2013; Garavand et al. 2016). This poses relevant unsolved problems both to academia and management given that adoption and implementation are very different phases of technology uptake and are both likely to be affected by hospital contextual factors (Esmaeilzadeh et al. 2011) (Varabyova et al. 2017). In other words, the factors underlying successful technologies are not only those leading to their swift acquisition and introduction in the organization, but also those capable of creating the conditions that favor their effective and safe use in time (Grossi et al. 2016).

A recent study has investigated such contextual determinants and has detected four main families of contextual items able to exert an impact on the effective implementation of health technologies (Grossi et al. 2019). The first family includes the hospital's infrastructure and architecture. Dimensions such as hospital size, hospital location and teaching vs. non-teaching status may exert an impact on the implementation of a technology. Also, the affiliation to some universities or to a multi-hospital network is associated to technology implementation. Importantly, the hospital's organizational chart (e.g., whether it is organized across transversal clinical pathways or not) must necessarily be at the basis of any consideration concerning the adoption of costly health technologies. These must be coherent with the working flows and assignment of responsibilities deriving from these charts.

Second, the hospital's availability of financial resources may play a key role too. Financial support and adequate budgeting are of the utmost importance for successful technology implementation. Resources are identified as a barrier when hospitals face difficulties in obtaining funding for high-cost technology. The absence of a budget that is coherent with organizational units' technological assets may hinder the possibility of using them in concrete. Cost issues and lack of reimbursement policies are the main cause of a sub-optimal use. Although intuitive in principle, this finding has further implications than the mere ascertainment that a hospital with more resources is advantaged in technology implementation. Indeed, implications concern the internal distribution of resources and their coherence with organizational units' technological assets. This, in turn, provides food for thought on the consequences of misaligning health technologies and budgets within or across organizational units.

Third, leadership and managerial styles may exert a relevant impact. A persistent and sustained leadership by top management is a key element to implement technologies successfully. Distant management may lead to a lack of detailed understanding of the tasks involved in patient care by operators as well as of the overall need of implementing technologies in specific ways. Technologies should be introduced in participative ways. Although an excessive decentralization of responsibilities to lower levels may hinder implementation, a "bottom-up" approach is usually more successful. Top management should play the role of "mediator" of professionals, by involving those at all levels - including nurses and representatives of all final users of the technology. This provides interesting implications in terms of managerial styles, suggesting an increased effectiveness of attitudes that approach a concern for people rather than a concern for results (Blake and Mouton 2016).

Fourth, human resource management tools are key in technology implementation. Human resource management is crucial across all its typical phases. In the first place, in the phase of staff supply and planning, due to the need of defining new roles, including those in charge of supporting the changes needed to implement the technology. Insufficient or inadequate human resources, staff shortages, lack of staff recruitment and contractual tensions are all barriers to technology implementation. Moreover, human resource management is also essential to plan education. To use a given technology effectively, it is often necessary to undergo an appropriate training program and many studies underline that the inability of satisfying training needs is a major barrier to implementation. Although education may be a time-consuming activity (Szydlowski and Smith 2009; Struik et al. 2014) and should be planned cautiously (Bomba and Land 2006), training programs are usually considered among the most important determinants of effective technology implementation. Nevertheless, not only training in a strict sense but also "general communication" may play a key role. Indeed, the use of a health technology may cause an extra workload or a perceived waste of time, inducing utilizers to use it against their will, in sub-optimal ways (Varonen, Kortteisto, and Kaila 2008; Nanji et al. 2009; Dharampal et al. 2016; Debono et al. 2017). In this scenario, it is important that human resource management tools are coherent with the hospital's organizational and technological asset and lead professionals to "accept" the technology, addressing their concerns, including those related to changes in consolidated ways of working.

In conclusion, although health technology assessment is attentive in capturing the effects of technologies on multiple domains (including the organizational one), the inverse relationship, i.e., how organizational, managerial, or contextual factors may affect the implementation of a health technology is still less explored. Yet, understanding these phenomena is a key priority for hospitals given that they must foresee the effects of technologies in their specific setting, considering their own specific characteristics. Put in other terms, such an analysis provides hospital managers with a deeper awareness of the possible "gaps" to be covered to ensure an excellent context to potentially successful health technologies, enabling them to positively affect hospital performance. Moreover, this allows them to clearly foresee the contribution of health technologies to the implementation of their hospital's strategy.

3.5. MULTIPLE CASE STUDIES TO ASSESS THE ROLE OF HOSPITAL CONTEXTUAL FACTORS ON TECHNOLOGY IMPLEMENTATION: A STUDY WITHIN THE EUROPEAN PROJECT IMPACT HTA

Within the European project IMPACT HTA (IMPACT HTA, 2021), two case studies were carried out at two university hospitals, to assess the role of hospital contextual factors on health technology implementation. The hospitals were the Agostino Gemelli University hospital in Rome, Italy and the Odense University Hospital, Denmark.

The Agostino Gemelli University hospital in Rome is the second largest general hospital in Italy, with 1,575 beds. This setting was chosen because of its relevant dimensions and complexity, combined to the very modern technologies it has adopted. The hospital is currently organized into 21 areas grouped into 8 departments which are responsible for coordinating all clinical, training and research activities within their boundaries. It uses clinical pathways systematically to map, integrate and assess every phase of providing care for key health pathologies. In 2015, almost 95,000 patients were hospitalized, and more than 45,000 surgical operations were conducted, while 80,000 patients were treated in the emergency department. Since 2015, the hospital has hosted one of the largest and newest hybrid operating theatres in Europe.

The interviews concerning the asset of contextual factors of the hospital and their effects on the use of technology and on performance produce evidence of a quickly evolving scenario. In particular, the Gemelli hospital is organized in a rather traditional way, with seven clinical directorates hierarchically subordinated to the Chief Medical Officer. Each clinical directorate includes various clinical wards and is generally quite autonomous in managing its resources and staff. Nevertheless, important organizational innovations have been implemented to pursue a strategic plan of organizational change, aimed at shifting towards a more horizontal organizational chart. First, many resources have been centralized and are shared across directorates. The most important example is the central operating theatre, which is led by a team of professionals who assign time slots to directorates, based on the priorities of efficiency and operating room saturation. Another example concerns nurses, who are led centrally by a dedicated function, which assigns professionals to directorates both based on their individual key competencies as well as pursuing effective and efficient allocations.

Second, the hospital has introduced a formal unit responsible for designing and managing clinical pathways for the major pathologies it treats. Currently, the pathways implemented are over 60. The creation of clinical pathways around a disease requires multi-disciplinary teams led by the clinical pathway unit and made up of representatives of all the major professionals involved in their different stages. This means that multi-disciplinarity is given both by the different clinical directorates involved (i.e., different clinical fields) as well as by the different types of professionals (e.g., physicians, surgeons, nurses). Through a permanent negotiation process, the pathway is formalized, and its performance indicators (and targets) are set. This means that a "transversal" evaluation integrates the typical setting-oriented one, with process indicators integrating the traditional clinical and financial ones (although the latter still play a much higher role in the overall performance evaluation). The team shares responsibility in the achievement of the expected results of performance. Although budgets are still assigned to clinical directorates and not to transversal clinical pathways, the participative nature of their teams makes it easier to commit clinical directorates to common objectives.

The hospital has formalized a human resource management function which plays a relevant role within the organization, functioning as a strategic partner to top management. The HRM function is responsible for designing and providing training initiatives to staff, but does so in cooperation with the requirements and suggestions coming from clinical directorates and from the nursing unit (which is independent from clinical directorates). Moreover, the HRM function has initiated a massive project of competency modelling, aimed at mapping and monitoring the set of competencies present and needed in most key managerial positions. This allows a timely assessment of possible discrepancies between the *as-is* and the *to-be* situations, and allows to adapt training strategies consequently. Nevertheless, this effort is still relatively recent and items such as seniority and formal appointments to positions are still the main drivers of career advancement and financial gratification.

The contextual characteristics of the Gemelli hospital are held to play a key role in its overall performance. In particular, its organizational chart, based on clinical directorates, is held to have a direct impact on the excellency reputation the hospital has built, with outstandingly high scientific competencies that distinguish its professionals. In other terms, this model is held to improve a "learning and growth" perspective, which can be measured, for example, through indicators such as number of scientific publications, number of presentations in international conferences, number of patents registered. The efforts of centralizing relevant resources is held to have a strong impact on efficiency, on utilization rates and on the financial dimension. In particular, ever since the introduction of the central operating theatre, the hospital has experienced much higher saturation rates than in the past, cutting wastes and relative costs dramatically. Moreover, the current organizational asset has variable effects on patient-centeredness. If on one side the patients who belong to a clinical pathway experience an integrated and coordinated experience of care, on the other, those who are not inserted into a pathway may still experience rather fragmented moments of care. This is why the hospital is investing massively in the creation of integrated pathways.

In reference to clinicians' perception of enablers and barriers to a fully effective implementation and use of health technologies, there emerge two recurrent issues. In the first place and in reference to surgical equipment, physicians state that the actual access to modern technologies is frequently tied to the "power" and charisma of clinical directors. In other terms, depending on their negotiation and charismatic abilities, there may exist drastic differences in the amount and quality of modern health technologies introduced within the clinical directorate, as well as the actual opportunity of sharing their use between senior and junior physicians. Yet, these discrepancies seem to have been mitigated since the introduction of a hospital-based HTA unit, which introduced a shared (across departments) technological strategy and an accountable use of health technologies investments. In other words, the traditional "power" of clinical directors could be interpreted as an enabler or barrier to health technology depending on his/her charisma and power of negotiation with the hospital's top management. This (positive or negative) effect is, however, mitigated by the hospital-based HTA unit, which increases equity in the introduction of technologies across the various directorates.

A second recurrent perspective is that there persists a major difficulty in implementing health technologies effectively due to a high cultural resistance from operators and an inadequate "understanding" of the tools' functioning and usefulness. This means that although "useful" tools are indeed introduced within the hospital to enhance its switch towards horizontal organizational models, these may not reach their full potential given the cultural rigidity of operators, tied to setting-centric accountability approaches. The impression of respondents is that the transformation from a vertical to a mixed organizational chart needs further support in terms of training and committing healthcare professionals, who tend to perceive the new technologies as time consuming, without necessarily grasping their overall utility.

Odense University Hospital is the largest and most specialized hospital in Southern Denmark, with 1,039 beds. More than 35 different medical specialties are represented in it, among which cardiology, clinical genetics and orthopedic surgery, and the hospital is well known for its innovative approach to technology use, implementation, and development. Every year more than 40.000 surgical operations are performed, and 104.000 patients discharged from the hospital.

The hospital is organized in a traditional vertical department structure which is however mitigated by shared progressive patient settings (e.g., common settings among departments which host patients with similar intensity of care needs). This is the case, for example, of a separate building within the hospitals' campus aimed at hosting patients that are no longer in need of intensive assistance. Moreover, although departments are assigned with their own staffed beds, a "flexible culture" was introduced to re-allocate beds across departments in case of need. Furthermore, the hospital has introduced transversal clinical pathways, especially for oncological diseases. In each pathway, each patient is assigned with a reference person, who is responsible for assuring a timely access to settings and exams and an overall fluidity of the pathway's implementation. Nevertheless, clinical pathways are not formally in possess of their own budget or beds. This means that in terms of resources, they still depend on vertical departments. Rather, they can be seen as structured and sustained collaborations of different professionals who still respond to vertical centers of responsibility.

Human Resource Management has designed career ladders along the various responsibilities that can be held withing departments although, given the fact that the hospital is a university hospital, an academic/research track ladder is alternative to the typical managerial one and is, possibly, even more prestigious.

The hospital disposes of an HTA unit which has the objective of supporting management in decision-making concerning technology adoption and use. Formally, final decisions are taken by a board of medical directors in top managerial positions. Nevertheless, the hospital's culture is more and more moving towards shared decision-making processes, which increase the weight of the opinion and the degree of accountability of departments and final users. The hospital-based HTA unit is also more and more called to intervene in support of departments and of their responsibility on overall quality achievement.

The hospital does not face relevant challenges in the implementation of routine medical devices through incremental processes of change. Professionals' competencies are perfectly adequate and in general they are willing to sustain continuous improvement. Nevertheless, issues may arise in the implementation of larger and more challenging health technologies, which imply radical forms of change in daily activities. This, again, is not because of professionals' competencies which, on the contrary, are likely to constitute an enabling factor to technology uptake, but rather to inadequate or incoherent funding. In particular, the problem lies in funding allocated in organizational units to implement the changes required by new technologies. These, usually, imply new procedures or complementary activities that require *ad hoc* funding. This incoherence between technology's implications and their funding has put the hospital in a situation in which only around 10% of technologies in the development projects are then concretely implemented in the hospital.

This aspect probably represents the most relevant barrier to technology implementation.

3.6. INFORMATION COMMUNICATION TECHNOLOGY TOOLS

3.6.1. Managing Usability, Integration, and Accessibility of ICT Systems

The information communication technology (ICT) system of a hospital is key in planning, measuring, assessing, and driving its performance. To do so effectively, hospitals need a set of complete and coherent data. Moreover, although hospitals may aim at implementing "ideal" ICT systems in theory, in practice they are always affected by internal and external constraints that cannot be overlooked (Arvanitis and Loukis 2015). In reference to external ones, for example, a hospital should not disregard the main ICT tools adopted by the other actors of its network or in the geographical area in which it operates. In terms of internal ones, it must seek an overall coherence of communication systems among hospital units and responsibility centers.

As mentioned previously, patients are more and more frequently in need of assistance that is built around transversal pathways that "cross" more clinical directorates. Nevertheless, although they have updated their organizational charts accordingly, many hospitals fail in ensuring smooth communication flows across their departments and units. This is in part due to the frequent "handoffs" occurring between departments, which may cause delays, errors, or unnecessary duplications of activities. The main limit of hospitals in which this sort of issue arises systematically, is that no one can take responsibility for the *overall* pathway of patients. Rather, each unit, each department, each team, is accountable for its own *part* of the pathway. This phenomenon, which may depend on various causes, is surely sustained by ICT systems that are designed in a fragmented way (Locatelli et al. 2010). Although distinct from each other, departments, clinical wards, and units are likely to need common information on one hand, and to feed common datasets on the other (Hurlen et al. 2010). Whether clinical or administrative in nature, this data must be made available when needed to whom it is needed. In many hospitals, units still have relatively autonomous ICT systems or procedures that are carried out in a rather disjoint way from the rest of the organization (Lee, Ramayah, and Zakaria 2011). An ICT system which does not assure the availability of clear and shared information across units and across all the various functional areas of the hospital, is likely to eventually lead to messy information flows and a scarce control over the contribution of each unit to hospital performance. This, in turn, means providing a weak support to top and middle managers, called to take both strategic and operative decisions, while not being fully informed on the current strengths and weaknesses of their organization.

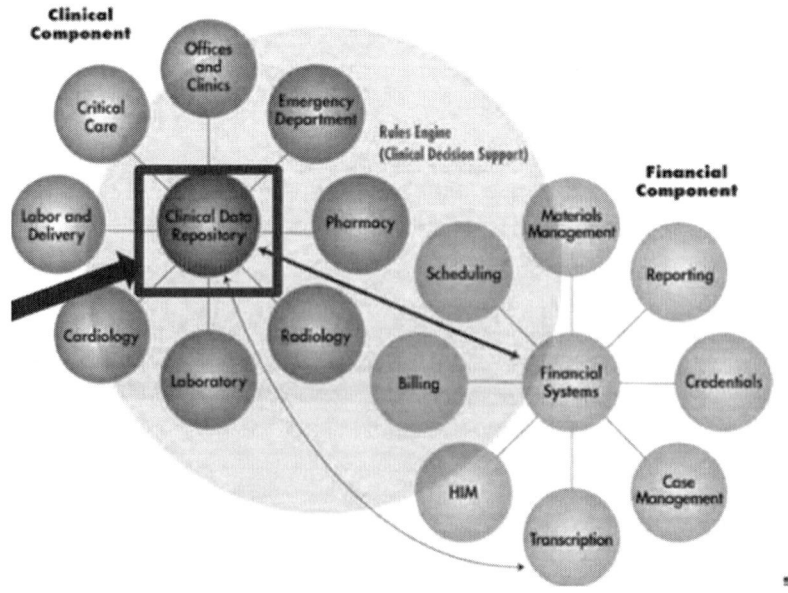

Source: Ferrara 2020.

Figure 12. A representation of integrated data repositories.

Moreover, this holds true not only within hospitals, but also across hospitals and other clinical settings (e.g., other hospitals, local health units, nursing homes) which are jointly responsible for providing assistance to patients along their continuum of care. With the evolution of digital technology and the boost of new solutions of e-health and m-health (Vukovic et al. 2018; Leung and Chen 2019; Hallberg and Salimi 2020), the settings in need of joint forms of communication and data exchange are even more than in the past, including, by now, patients' homes too. The challenge of creating fluid communication flows not only within but also across settings and organizations is a major topic in the healthcare scenario worldwide (Miller et al. 2018). Such integration may have to occur across all actors of the same network, in the same area or also in the same region or country. Although these actors are usually peculiar (characterized by a specific social mission), diverse (in organizational, clinical, technological terms, for example) and frequently autonomous (disposing of their own identity, budgets, and resources), they are indeed in need of sharing information. For example, many healthcare systems experience a dangerous lack of information exchange between hospitals and general practitioners (Essex et al. 1991). If a patient is visited by his/her general practitioner, only seldom is there a structured way of sharing information with the hospital that will then take him/her in charge, and vice-versa. This means that precious information risks being lost or used late due to a lack of coherence between the hospital's and the general practitioner's ICT system.

This problem has negative consequences also on the availability of big data at the system's level. Fragmented information hinders forms of overall data assessment and may slow down key initiatives to improve the assistance to patients. In this scenario, clinical data repositories are key in grouping and managing data provided by multiple sources. These are "aggregations of granular patient-centric health data usually collected by multiple-source ICT systems and intended to support multiple uses" ("Definition of Clinical Data Repository (CDR) - Gartner Information Technology Glossary" 2021).

Clinical data repositories have the potential of bringing together huge quantities of information coming from very different sources, including clinical data collected by Apps and wearable devices, which are by now so commonly used (Park, Cho, and Chung 2011). Although a single information system for all settings and for all types of information is not realistic in practice, all this different data can indeed merge into clinical data repositories that are compatible with different ICT systems, apps, devices, and codings. This approach would enable this information convergence without the need to invest a great amount of money in converting pre-existing information systems. Data repositories may be just as useful for administrative data, both at the organizational and at the inter-organizational levels (Smith et al. 2018) and, in their extreme development, may be integrated with clinical ones.

Beyond the adoption and implementation of data repositories at the organizational and system levels, some other ICT tools are currently transforming the information communication systems of many countries. These tools, which are leading healthcare systems towards integrated, patient-centered approaches, include electronic health records (Ben-Zion, Pliskin, and Fink 2014). These are digital versions of patients' paper charts which, in their integrated forms, are accessible to different professionals in different moments of the continuum of care (Melnick et al. 2020). In other words, they are real-time, patient-centered records that make information available instantly and securely to authorized users. Although they do contain medical and treatment histories of patients, they can include additional data that goes beyond standard clinical data collection. For example, they may contain a patient's medical history, diagnoses, laboratory and test results, medications, radiology images, treatment plans, immunization dates, allergies. Again, this integration of information may concern the hospital level, by connecting, for example, different clinical directorates, laboratories, medical imaging facilities. However, fully developed electronic health records have the potentiality of transforming communication systems *across* settings in a decisive way (Giordanengo et al. 2016). Indeed, all the clinicians involved in a patient's clinical pathway in any setting and in any moment of the patient's life, may potentially have access to the full array of information concerning the patient, with paramount implications on the effectiveness of his/her clinical decisions. A high investment on electronic health records would eventually lead to inter-organizational, inter-regional and possibly international integration, fostering patient mobility within and across countries (Elliott et al. 2012).

It is very important that this digital transformation is carried out simultaneously with the organizational ones aimed at fostering patient-centered care. If these two dimensions do not move along together, new organizational models are bound to fail or only partially succeed in their intents. This is because of the bottlenecks that would arise due to fragmented information, able to hinder the fluidity on which the model depends. On the other hand, this digital transition would not only represent a necessary item of a broader organizational one, but would also set the bases for the systematic collection of exhaustive, reliable and timely data for a wide range of studies, going from epidemiological ones, to those assessing costs and effectiveness of strategies of care.

3.6.2. Monitoring Safety through the ICT System

The ICT system must be able to guarantee full safety to all the stakeholders involved in its implementation. ICT systems must be designed so as to overcome or mitigate several risks, each of which constitutes a concrete threat to the system's adequacy. Figure 13 reports a list of risks connected to the use of ICT tools. It also reports a list of corresponding aspects to be pursued when designing the ICT system in the first place or while assessing systems that are already in use.

Taking into account the risks associated to the use of an ICT system means planning and arranging various organizational and managerial aspects accordingly. For example, hospitals should formalize the position of a responsible for the ICT safety with adequate power to intervene proactively, as well as reactively, to safety incidents. Hospitals should dispose of a structured plan to enhance ICT safety, as well as carrying out periodic audits and assessments of the concrete degree of safety in the organization. Moreover, hospitals are likely to benefit from a close cooperation between the ICT unit and the clinical risk unit, which should jointly be accountable for enhancing smooth and safe procedures. It is also important that data are systematically and exclusively uploaded and stored in official repositories (Englebright, Aldrich, and Taylor 2014). Finally, it is important for hospitals to dispose of disaster-recovery technologies and a well-structured recovery plan to be adopted in case of unexpected emergencies (Lee and Guster 2012).

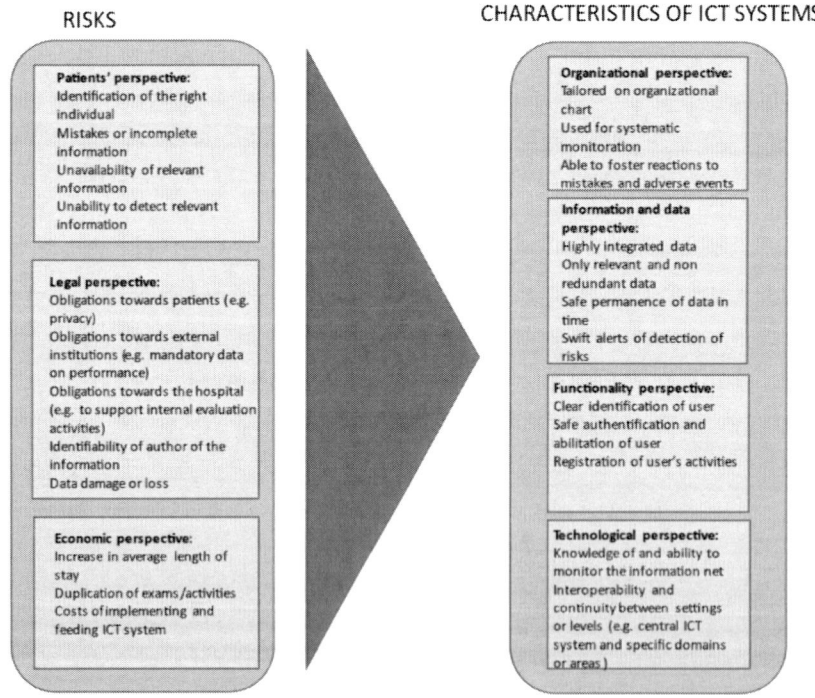

Source: Author's re-elaboration from Ferrara 2020.

Figure 13. Examples of risks associated to hospital ICT systems and of their desirable characteristics.

3.6.3. Rethinking Communication Systems in Managing Chronic Pathologies

The more chronic conditions spread within the populations of developed countries, the more healthcare systems must adapt so as to guarantee assistance in the most appropriate settings, without increasing costs excessively. If on one hand, chronicity implies that many activities can be carried out in primary settings or also in patients' homes, on the other, this trend may nurture the risk of increasing dispersion phenomena in various ways (Muijen et al. 1992). Moreover, if not well designed and implemented through effective communication systems, a clinical pathway may result in patients feeling "abandoned" in all those moments in which they are not directly involved in an activity within a hospital or physical setting (Heerema-Poelman, Stuive, and Wempe 2013). This, in turn, may lead to issues such as poor compliance with therapies, causing both waste and worse clinical outcomes. A second issue concerns the dispersion of relevant clinical information (e.g., lab exams, vital parameters), which risks not being collected in a structured and systematic way, leading to situations in which important information is missing when taking important clinical decisions (Cavalleri, Morstabilini, and Reni 2005). Finally, this may increase the risk of not detecting a sudden worsening of the health status or even an emergency in a timely manner (Brown et al. 2006). If patients are not continuously "involved" in a clinical pathway, awareness of such worsening may be very delayed, and physicians may not detect them on time. This could produce deleterious effects both on patients' health as well as on the costs incurred by the healthcare system to care for them.

In this scenario, it is paramount to introduce information and communication approaches that guarantee full and timely access to all the relevant information concerning patients by all the professionals involved in the provision of care at different stages of their clinical pathway. As mentioned, professionals should have access and feed shared health records, with updated information at any moment, in all settings. For chronic conditions, a care manager (who could be the patient's general practitioner) should ideally design a personalized monitoring plan and identify events or critical situations that should generate immediate alerts and pro-actively require medical intervention (Alhuwail and Koru 2016). Innovative ICT solutions for the provision of care to chronic patients are more and more oriented towards pro-actively alerting (e.g., via mail, via sms) patients about the actions they should carry out (e.g., taking a medicine, measuring blood pressure) so as to increase compliance and, also, returning clinical information to professionals swiftly, deriving it directly from the electronical devices used.

This sort of communication approach introduces unprecedented advantages in our healthcare systems. Patients can easily be in touch with professionals in any moment and always feel taken care of across their continuum of care. They can feel reassured that they can always turn to someone in case of need and rely on a system that is constantly present. Data is shared among different professionals (e.g., general practitioner, hospital doctor, care/case manager) and these can all interact or provide their point of view in all the main episodes of clinical decision-making. The system automatically generates alerts to emphasize anomalous parameters and supports pro-active and timely interventions by the whole team of professionals. Professionals can be in touch with patients and modify their treatments according to the most recent information available, reducing waiting lists for visits and improving timeliness, effectiveness, and patient-satisfaction.

Although potentially very promising, these technological revolutions require important investments in terms of acquisition, implementation, and training both of staff and patients (Seto et al. 2019). Moreover, the risk of, paradoxically, further fragmenting information is concrete if this transition is not driven by a central actor. Although it is unlikely that a hospital may drive this transition on its own (although it may indeed play a very proactive role not only within its boundaries but also in its surrounding territory), hospitals must indeed invest in adapting quickly to these changes. This implies, in turn, re-shaping the internal ICT system so as to be fully integrated with the information flows coming from outside.

3.6.4. Linking Communication Systems to Hospital Performance

The ICT system and the extent to which it is correctly implemented are likely to exert an important effect on various aspects of hospital performance. In the first place, on its economic and financial dimension due to its capability of supporting managerial accounting tools effectively as well as of supporting the provision of services in cheaper and more cost-effective ways (Arvanitis and Loukis 2015). Second, it has a clear effect on the efficiency and effectiveness of hospital activities and processes (Langer et al. 2014). If supported by timely and reliable information, activities can be carried out quickly, without redundancies and in the most effective possible way. Moreover, and related to this point, the ICT system can highly affect safety and the overall health of patients (as well as of staff) (Langer et al. 2014). If processes are carried out smoothly, positive effects will be reached in terms of final clinical efficacy. More in general, it is possible to state that the ICT system too should be thought of a strategic tool that can support hospitals in reaching their main goals. ICT can support but also drive strategic change by contributing to a continuous and sustained improvement of the services provided and of overall organizational performance.

3.7. HUMAN RESOURCE MANAGEMENT TOOLS

3.7.1. The New Strategic Role of the Human Resource Management Function

One of the possibly most important factors in determining hospital success is given by its human resources (Kellner et al. 2016). In a global scenario in which the governance system of a hospital must guarantee the attainment of high levels of both effectiveness and efficiency, professionals' ability of implementing the strategic changes the sector is facing is key. Consequently, this implies that the HRM function is by now more and more conceived as co-responsible (with other top managerial figures) not only for implementing hospital strategies, but also for co-designing them in the first place.

More specifically, HRM is by now frequently assuming the role of strategic partner of the upper echelon, and is responsible for planning, implementing, and monitoring strategies through the development and sustainment of the appropriate competencies of professionals. Given that hospital organizational charts are changing, professional roles must evolve accordingly. New organizational models imply the emergence of new professional roles, and frequently these imply the need of a new set of competencies and attitudes. New organizational units, new procedures, new technologies, and new roles in general are all highly dependent on the presence of professionals who understand them, accept them, and can implement them effectively (Gile, Buljac-Samardzic, and Klundert 2018). In this way, HRM should no longer be seen as an administrative function with operational tasks only, but rather as a component of the hospital's strategic managerial alliance, with pervasive responsibilities across the whole organization. HRM is therefore shifting from a "linear" relationship with top management (and its strategy), to an "interdependent" one (Shipton et al. 2016). In the first case it is top management that determines the hospital's strategy, and this affects its organizational structure and, in turn, HRM action in a top-down perspective. In the second case, there exist a mutual causal relationship and HRM is affected but also affects organizational models and strategies (Figure 14).

In concrete, this means that HRM is called to assess key professional positions across the hospital and assure their coherence with the overall strategy and trends of change. Moreover, it must guarantee that professionals allocated to these positions are indeed capable of carrying out their tasks and of reaching their objectives. Finally, HRM must monitor these equilibria in time and adapt its own interventions swiftly in all situations in which discrepancies between expected and achieved outcomes arise.

Table 3. The phases of human resource management in hospitals and their contribution to the implementation of horizontal organizational solutions

HRM Phase	Brief description	Contribution to new horizontal organizational trends
Selection	Selecting new staff from outside the hospital	During the selection phase, the hospital has its unique chance to introduce within its boundaries people in possess of the competencies needed to implement new organizational solutions. If these are present on the job market, this may be cheaper than training all professionals inside the hospital.
Allocation	Allocating hospital staff to new professional positions	Many competencies may be present within the hospital but not used at their best potential. HRM can re-allocate professionals through internal vertical and horizontal career ladders, so as to reach the best match between people's attitudes and the positions they cover.
Training	Developing competencies during people's professional life	Training may be thought of as a continuous process that must be deeply interconnected with the competencies needed to implement new organizational solutions. Before acquiring competencies from outside, it is frequently convenient to develop them within the hospital. Training paths must be clearly associated to career paths and must be designed strategically.
Evaluation	Evaluating professionals and their achievements	Evaluation is a complex process that includes the evaluation of positions, people (competencies) and of performance. Professionals should be systematically evaluated so as to timely intervene in case of discrepancies between desirable and concrete achievements. This phase is strictly connected to the training one (which intervenes in case of detection of discrepancies) and to the compensation one.
Compensation	Compensating professionals in just and equitable ways	Monetary and non-monetary compensation must assure just and fair treatments to professionals. These must also constitute an effective incentive in implementing behaviors that are instrumental to the achievement of strategic goals.

Source: Author's elaboration.

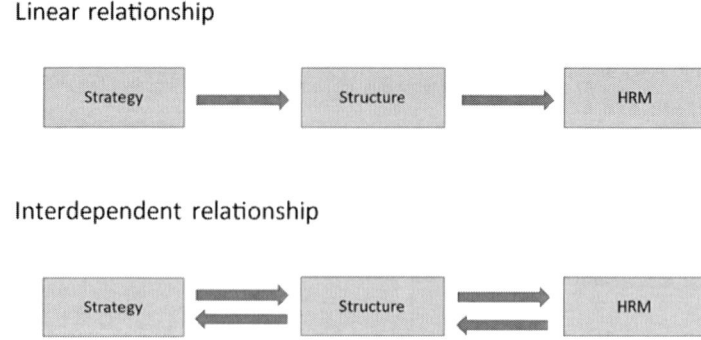

Source: Shipton et al. 2016.

Figure 14. A representation of the "linear" and of the "interdependent" relationship between hospital strategy and the human resource management function.

More specifically, all the typical phases of people management must converge towards this objective (Fanelli, Lanza, and Zangrandi 2018). The processes of hiring, allocating, training, and evaluating people should all tend towards the strategic imprint of the hospital. Each of these HRM phases must be coherent with each other and must be linked to the overall objective of guaranteeing the presence of the "right competencies in the right place." Table 3 summarizes the typical phases of HRM as well as their contribution to the implementation of patient-centered care.

3.7.2 Managing New Professional Roles

Hospital professional roles are facing deep transformations. Given that hospitals are shifting towards horizontal organizational models and are systematically involved in inter-organizational forms of provision of care, many professional roles are evolving accordingly. The deep revisitation of a culture that was traditionally based on responsibility units rigidly anchored to specific settings, to a more "shared" (across settings and teams) vision of responsibility (Rosemond et al. 2012), are probably at the basis of this evolution. This deep transformation is necessarily accompanied by a transformation in professional vocations and roles with, for example, many clinical figures assuming more and more managerial responsibilities compared to the past (Norrish and Rundall 2001). Moreover, the actual meaning of managerial responsibility is changing, in coherence with the new configurations of healthcare organizations. Necessarily, the whole "equilibrium" of responsibilities across the wide range of professionals in hospitals must be re-considered.

Generally, key clinical roles in hospitals can be assigned to one of the following families (FIASO 2021):

- "purely professional" roles: these are those roles in which professionals exert their clinical role in a dominant way and only marginally or occasionally are required to carry out administrative activities. The latter are, in any case, to be intended as in support of their core clinical work;
- "setting managerial" roles: these are managerial roles that are strictly connected to a specific unit or setting within the hospital (e.g. a department, a clinical ward, the operating theatre). These professionals are in charge of guaranteeing the overall effectiveness and efficiency of all the activities carried out within their unit and are responsible towards top management of the good use of the resources they are assigned with;
- "pathway or process managerial" roles: these professionals are in charge of the effectiveness of overall transversal processes that concern different organizational units either sequentially or simultaneously.

Table 4 provides some examples of professionals typically belonging to each of the three families.

In such large and complex organizations such as hospitals, the different features and high number of roles to be managed make it challenging to pursue full coherence among them, and between them and the hospital's strategy. Moreover, it is well known that forms of resistance to change are potentially able to frustrate even the most thoughtful and coherent plans of development of hospital professional roles (Brunetto, Farr-Wharton, and Shacklock 2011). Therefore, it is of paramount importance to introduce strategies of change in thoughtful and participative ways, both at the hospital and at the policy making levels. Implementing a new professional role implies an active management of different features.

Table 4. A classification of professional roles in hospitals

Type of role	Physicians	Nurses
Purely professional role	Clinical doctor	Nurse dedicated to assistance to patients
Setting managerial role	Clinical Director, Head of Clinical Ward	Department Head of Nurses, Head of week surgery, Manager of Operating Theatre
Pathway or process managerial role	Case Manager (physician); Responsible of Clinical Pathway	Case Manager (nurse), Care Manager, Discharge Manager, Risk Manager

Source: Author's adaptation from Cicchetti 2019.

First, it must be clarified which responsibilities are attributed to the role and which tasks it will have to carry out. Although obvious in principle, failing in defining this accurately may lead to forms of role ambiguity and/or role conflict (Tunc and Kutanis 2009). Role conflict occurs when people disagree about the expectations on a given role or have difficulties satisfying them because their duties are unclear, complicated, or disagreeable. The result is that individuals experiencing role conflict are frustrated due to contrasting expectations on them. Role ambiguity denotes uncertainty about the actual expectations, behaviors or even responsibilities within a given role. It occurs when organizational factors (e.g., rapidly changing organizational structures, job feedback systems) are inadequately communicated or inexistent (Bowling et al. 2017).

Second, competency profiles must be clearly attributed to each role, so as to drive all HRM phases towards the acquisition of the "right person for the right position". Activities such as, for example, staff selection, allocation or training must all converge towards the common objecti ensuring that professionals are able to carry out their job effectively and with success. Therefore, they should all be tailored around clear competency profiles that are coherent with what strategically expected from the professional position in the first place.

Finally, tools to assess the performance of professionals covering key hospital roles must be defined. These should be tailored on the specific features of the position itself. Each of these three aspects must necessarily be coherent if the hospital wants to guarantee a smooth and successful implementation of new professional roles. The following section describes a case study carried out at the inter-organizational level in Italy, aimed at defining competency profiles of two key figures in hospitals.

3.8. Driving New Professional Roles through Competencies: The Experience of the Italian Federation of Hospitals and Healthcare Organizations (FIASO)

Although the general trends of change in healthcare organizations appear rather clear, there seems to persist a very worrying lag in the system's capability of "updating" professional roles accordingly (Lega and De Pietro 2005). Although important efforts both at policy and organizational levels do exist (Mitchell and Boak, 2009), the general feeling is that phenomena such as role conflict and role ambiguity are extremely frequent in the sector (Kurunmaki and Kurunmaki 1999).

A response to these problems is competency modeling, which focuses on addressing the personal attributes that are directly linked to an organization's objectives and strategy (Lievens, Sanchez, and Corte 2004). These personal characteristics are key predictors of professionals' effectiveness in carrying out their duties (Mcclelland 1973). In this scenario, a study was carried out by the Italian Federation of Hospitals and Healthcare Organizations (FIASO) to come up with competency profiles of key middle managerial figures in hospitals (FIASO 2021).

In a pilot phase of the study, two professional roles were investigated: Clinical Directors (CDs) and Head of Nurses (HNs) at hospital level. These are both of particular interest because hospitals' new organizational charts and cultures affect them emblematically. Hospitals' transition from vertical to horizontal models implies that on one hand CDs (physicians) are called to learn how to "share" some of the responsibilities that they traditionally held (Lega and De Pietro 2005). On the other hand, because of the increasing managerial role nurses cover and because of the higher relevance of horizontal responsibility units, HNs are called to re-negotiate nurses' role and to support or drive hospitals' re-organization (Gabutti and Cicchetti 2017). Indeed, deep re-negotiations of managerial responsibilities between physicians and nurses are currently taking place (Udlis and Mancuso 2015).

Within the framework of a broader study, this pilot investigation explored the ideal behavioral competencies of the two professional figures assessed. In close cooperation with the official Italian category associations of each professional figure, an analytical job description was written for both positions. Next, a "competencies dictionary" was used to assess the two ideal competency profiles, in coherence with the tasks and features expressed in the job descriptions. The dictionary, which consists of a list of key competencies with a specific definition thereof (hence the term dictionary), also included possible graduations of the "intensity" with which they may be possessed. For each professional figure, key competencies as well as their ideal level were identified. The category associations were warned about selecting a level that was reasonable and not unrealistic, so as to avoid the tendency of automatically selecting the higher levels of the scales. To be realistic, such levels should be coherent with the educational requirements mentioned in the job description as well as with the overall hierarchical position within the organization. Once the profiles were defined, they were both presented to a pool of Chief Executive Officers of Italian healthcare organizations for validation. The behavioral competencies selected for each profile are represented in Figure 15.

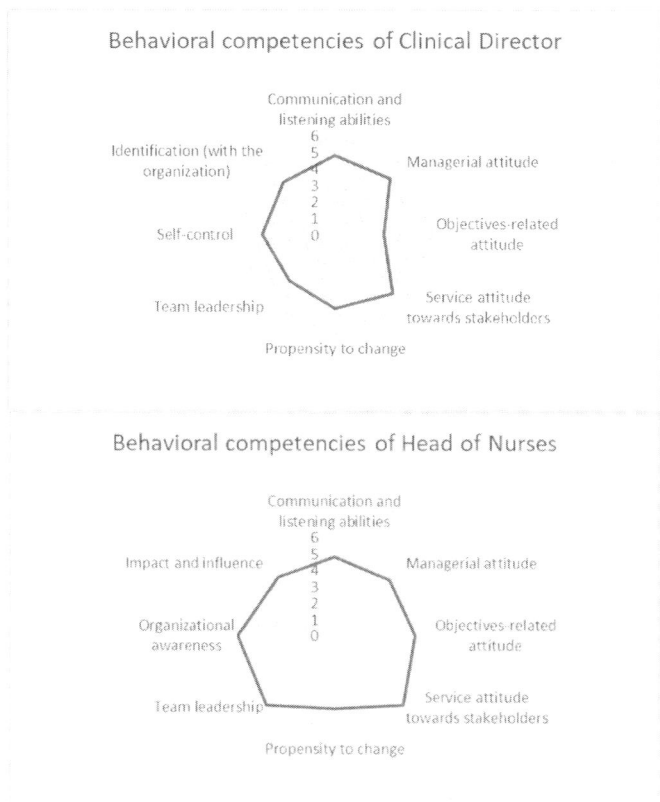

Source: FIASO 2021.

Figure 15. Key behavioral competencies of Clinical Directors and of Head of Nurses detected in the study by FIASO.

For both professionals it appears that communication and listening abilities are crucial. This suggests, according to the dictionary, that both figures are required to communicate in clear ways and to listen carefully to their interlocutors, asking frequently for feedbacks. Moreover, they should both be able to adopt the best communication tools and styles in every situation, including in moments of stress.

They should both develop a high managerial attitude, suggesting that they should be able to define and explain objectives, share and clarify performance standards as well as delegate the concrete ways in which priorities must be implemented. They should be able to achieve a high accountability and commitment of other individuals to reach the hospital's objectives. This is tied to the need of developing their objectives-related attitude, ensuring that the hospital's strategy is reached through the concrete achievement of specific operational objectives. In turn, this is also coherent with the requirement of top leadership competencies, having to lead large groups of highly skilled professionals, who must be committed to the achievement of common goals. Moreover, both figures are required to be in possess of a highly developed service attitude towards stakeholders. Although for both roles this is a priority, for the NC this competency is required at the top level, highlighting maybe the intrinsic nature of the nursing profession which is, by definition, focused on assisting patients. Nurse coordinators, for example, are required to solve patients' problems proactively, detecting them in advance and looking for solutions even before they are expressed. Finally, the two professionals are both required to develop their propensity to change, suggesting that they must be able to adapt their behaviors to changing situations swiftly, and that they need to decode events as soon as they take place, detecting their meanings and implications. This is coherent with the deep transformations their organizations are facing in this era.

On the other hand, there emerge some distinctive competencies for the two roles. The CD should develop competencies such as self-control and identification with the organization. The NC should rather develop his/her organizational awareness as well as impact and influence. This distinction appears quite in line with some peculiar traits of the two positions. CDs cover a position that is more formally rooted in hospitals' hierarchies. Their greater "power" implies they should always use it in the interest of organizations, by self-controlling themselves and recognizing the importance of organizational goals even more than professional ones. Although these features are clearly important for any managerial figure (and possibly for HNs too), they are distinctive of top managerial roles or of roles that are close to top ones. HNs, on the other hand, must develop their organizational awareness (i.e., awareness of how "things happen" in the hospital) and their ability of exerting an impact on people's way of working. This aspect is key for a position that enjoys a less formal and consolidated power within the hierarchy and must, therefore, sharpen the capacity of reaching objectives in alternative ways. If this cannot be done exclusively or predominantly through the exercise of power (i.e., by giving directives), given the still rising role of this profession, objectives must be reached through persuasion and impact, by convincing people to adopt the desired behaviors.

It is interesting to interpret the two competency profiles conjunctly, in the light of the new equilibria that are characterizing hospitals in our era. On one hand, the role of HNs is rapidly evolving, gaining significance and responsibility within the organizational framework. This can be seen thanks to the relevance of behavioral competencies which overlap, to a good extent, with those that are typically attributed to consolidated managerial figures such as CDs. On the other hand, though, HNs are indeed "new" professional figures that are still negotiating their role, in a very complex and rooted context. This means that their competency profile cannot coincide with that of CDs, who can benefit from "traditional" ways of exerting power. Rather, they must develop alternative competencies that compensate the lack of power in a strict sense. Therefore, the two profiles reflect the concrete scenario that is realistically present in many hospitals, as well as fostering individuals to contribute to re-shape our hospitals of the future.

3.8.3. Future Developments of Competency Modeling in Hospitals

Structured implementations of competency modeling may highly support hospitals in their daily as well as strategic activities. Competency modeling may positively affect all phases of HRM. For example, selection and allocation of staff may be driven by pre-determined competency profiles, guiding these phases towards the identification of those professionals who are most likely to succeed within a specific position. Traditional selection criteria may be integrated by additional ones, built on the set of competencies needed in a certain professional position. Assessing the "right competencies" should ideally involve both the assessment of technical and managerial/behavioral ones. This is key in organizational scenarios such as hospitals, in which the hybrid (clinical and managerial) features of roles are in urgent need of being combined and managed effectively (Giacomelli 2019). Competency modeling can drive training programs, which should be tailored or combined so as to cover the gaps in competencies detected in individuals or teams. Finally, the phases of evaluation and compensation too may be integrated with a component specifically built on the achievement and maintenance of the required competencies. In other words, the whole HRM cycle may be inspired by a preliminary map of the competencies for key roles or families of roles, so as to provide overall coherent and targeted interventions by the HRM function.

For example, building on the pilot study described in section 3.6., Clinical Directors and Head of Nurses share only part of their ideal characteristics. Although the two professionals come from very different backgrounds, some of their responsibilities are clearly similar. Both are responsible for managing large teams of highly skilled professionals and of leading their efforts towards organizational strategic performance. This explains the overlap of competencies between them. Both need high inter-personal abilities related to leadership and communication. Nevertheless, the competencies detected do differ insofar as the CD traditionally exerts more power and must "control" his or her use of it, while the HN needs to develop alternative persuasive techniques. In practical terms, this means that some steps of their training pathway may be thought in a joint way, while other characterizing skills may be developed in *ad hoc* training activities. At the organizational level, if this approach is adopted widely, all phases of HRM can be carried out in more efficient and effective ways (Calhoun et al. 2016). Training activities can be designed modularly and according to the hospital's desired map of competencies.

Defining competency profiles in this way may support both operational and strategic hospital activity. In the first case it does so by driving all HRM activities towards the desired profiles. In the second, it may proactively drive strategy implementation. If, for example, a hospital decides to abandon a rigid hierarchical organizational model to adopt more flexible, horizontal solutions, it will have to guarantee the right allocation of competencies across organizational units to avoid decoupling phenomena. On the other hand, professionals with the "right competencies" play an active role in affecting organizational strategies. If, for example, the nursing profession is shifting towards new managerial responsibilities, HNs play a key role in contributing to the re-definition of responsibility boundaries. Similarly, CDs must contribute to this change too. If such transition is a strategic priority for the hospital, highly skilled CDs who are, however, resistant to change, may constitute an insurmountable barrier to the success of the strategy. Hence, specific competencies may help foster the change that is "in the air".

3.8.4. Re-Shaping Hospital Career Ladders

Among the strategic implications of adopting a competency modeling approach, it is important to highlight that this is likely to exert a relevant impact on hospital career paths. This constitutes a key factor of transition when implementing organizational strategic change. Career paths should be designed and implemented in coherence with the main strategic plans of the hospital.

Career paths in the healthcare sector are traditionally distant from some of the main typical trends of change in hospitals and in other healthcare organizations (Parsons et al. 1997). The transition towards horizontal or matrix organizational models is frequently not supported by tailored career ladders (Gabutti, Mascia, and Cicchetti 2017). Indeed, it is common that these remain tied to traditional vertical steps, which hinder a true transition towards an increased accountability and role of horizontal/transversal organizational units. Moreover, the focus in climbing a career ladder in a hospital is usually that of gradually abandoning clinical responsibility in a strict sense, to shift towards managerial tasks and activities. This may lead to situations in which professionals feel forced to accept managerial responsibilities so as to advance in their career, although they feel naturally more inclined towards their professional (clinical) vocation (Gabutti 2019).

Section 3.8. presents a case-study of an innovative solution in the design of hospital career ladders of physicians and nurses in a Spanish hospital.

3.9. DESIGNING NEW CAREER LADDERS IN HOSPITAL CLINIC, BARCELONA

Hospital Clinic is a university hospital located in Barcelona, in the Region of Catalonia in Spain, owned by the Government of Catalonia and the University of Barcelona. It disposes of around 800 beds. Hospital Clinic is a tertiary hospital of Catalonia, as well as a part of the community health care of Barcelona Esquerra- literally the 'left part of Barcelona'. Until 1995 the hospital was organized following a 'traditional' organizational chart based on clinical departments, grouped into four divisions (medical, surgical, specialties, central services). In 1996 the hospital was completely re-organized in "institutes" or "centers" (which are vertical semi-autonomous diagnostic treatment areas) and in "units" (which are transversal process-oriented areas designed around a specific disease or pathology).

The hospital introduced a dual career system both for doctors and nurses. For each, both a professional and a managerial career ladder have been developed. The new system was designed in such a way as to recognize professionals' medical skills, qualifications, and experience through the advancement on the "professional career ladder" and to recognize and reward their leadership and managerial efforts through a "managerial career ladder". The various steps of the four career ladders are reported in Figures 16 and 17.

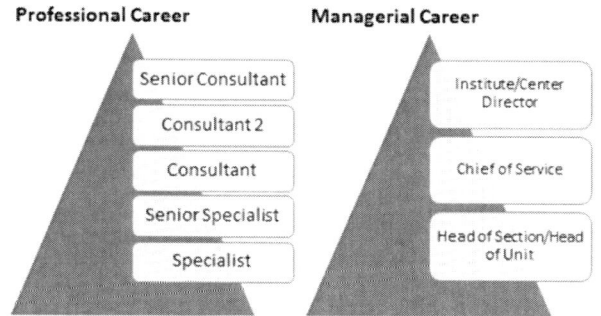

Source: Gabutti and Cicchetti 2017.

Figure 16. Parallel career ladders for physicians in Hospital Clinic.

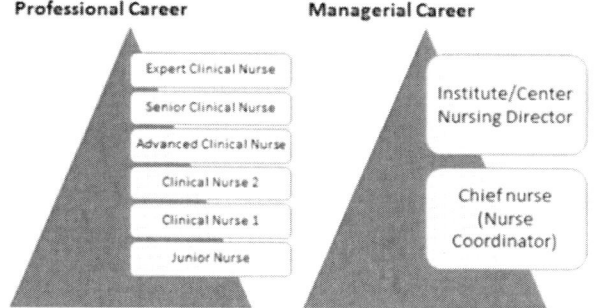

Source: Gabutti and Cicchetti 2017.

Figure 17. Parallel career ladders for nurses in Hospital Clinic.

In the professional careers of both physicians and nurses, a minimum of 5 years of experience in each position is required before being eligible for promotion. This is conferred by specific committees, made up of both apical and non-apical figures, so as to guarantee a participated decision-making process.

In the managerial tracks, one holds a position for 4 years, at the end of which an evaluation takes place by a nomination committee (again, made up of both apical and non-apical figures). Nurses on the managerial track also perform self-evaluations. In case of a positive assessment, the professional may advance to the next step. In general, assessments take into consideration managerial and leadership skills. There is always the option of interrupting this career to go back to the professional one. Moreover, to access specific managerial positions, it may be required to hold specific positions on the professional track.

There exists a formalized management by objectives[1] approach (Schnoor, Braehler, and Heyde 2019) for the managerial careers of physicians. Part of the salaries (around 15%) is tied to the extent to which the objectives are reached. Objectives usually concern dimensions related to budgets, assistance, and research. Compensation policies of physicians also include a sabbatical year. Since objectives are set for all the figures of the managerial track, each one of these may be held responsible in case they not reached. Responsibilities are indeed shared between vertical institutes and the horizontal units.

In general, nurses are not involved in many management by objectives initiatives. Objectives are usually not assigned to nurses (not even as a team), with the exception of nurses and technicians belonging to laboratories. Anyhow, the hospital is planning to extend the use of a management by objectives approach to all nurses (i.e., for positions on both the professional and the managerial tracks).

Conclusion

Managerial interventions, although different in nature and at times carried out by different professionals, must all be oriented towards pursuing transversal and integrated delivery of care. Managerial accounting tools must pursue shared (among professionals, among units, among organizations) accountability on the implementation of processes.

---

[1] Management by objectives is a strategic management model that aims to improve the performance of an organization by clearly defining objectives that are negotiated by both management and employees. According to the theory, having a shared role in goal setting and action plans, increases employee participation and commitment and aligns objectives across the organization.

Health technologies must be introduced in hospitals in ways that are coherent with organizational charts and, in general, with how processes are concretely carried out within them. It is therefore important to involve end-users in strategic decision making, in a bottom-up perspective. Information communication technology tools are key in assuring smooth and timely information across professionals, even more so if they are operating in different settings and in different moments. Human resource management tools are fundamental to develop the competencies needed to implement new organizational solutions effectively. All the typical phases of HRM must be built around this idea and must support the design of career pathways that truly incentivize the implementation of new models. To achieve this overall "harmony" in a hospital's managerial intervention, it is important to develop a strong, compact, and committed guidance at the top levels of the organization.

REFERENCES

"AdHopHTA | A New European Project on Hospital Based Health Technology Assessment." n.d. Accessed September 10, 2021. https://www.adhophta.eu/.

Alhuwail, D., and Koru, G. 2016. "Leveraging Health Information Technology for Fall-Risk Management in Home Care: A Qualitative Exploration of Clinicians' Perspectives." *Http://Dx.Doi.Org/10.1177/1084822316640266* 28 (4): 241–49. https://doi.org/10.1177/1084822316640266.

Arvanitis, S., and Loukis, E.N. 2015. "Investigating the Effects of ICT on Innovation and Performance of European Hospitals: An Exploratory Study." *The European Journal of Health Economics 2015 17:4* 17 (4): 403–18. https://doi.org/10.1007/S10198-015-0686-9.

Ben-Zion, R., Pliskin, N., and Fink, L. 2014. "Critical Success Factors for Adoption of Electronic Health Record Systems: Literature Review and Prescriptive Analysis." http://Dx.Doi.Org/10.1080/

10580530.2014.958024 31 (4): 296–312. https://doi.org/10.1080/10580530.2014.958024.

Blake, R. R., and Mouton, J. S. 2016. *Management by Grid® Principles or Situationalism: Which?* https://Doi.Org/10.1177/105960118100600404 6 (4): 439–55. https://doi.org/10.1177/105960118100600404.

Bomba, D., and Land, T. 2006. "The Feasibility of Implementing an Electronic Prescribing Decision Support System: A Case Study of an Australian Public Hospital." *Australian Health Review: A Publication of the Australian Hospital Association* 30 (3): 380–88. https://doi.org/10.1071/AH060380.

Bowling, N. A., Khazon, S., Alarcon, G. M., Blackmore, C. E., Bragg, C. B., Hoepf, M. R., Barelka, A., Kennedy, K., Wang, Q., and Li, H. 2017. *Building Better Measures of Role Ambiguity and Role Conflict: The Validation of New Role Stressor Scales.* https://Doi.Org/10.1080/02678373.2017.1292563 31 (1): 1–23. https://doi.org/10.1080/02678373.2017.1292563.

Brown, E. L., Raue, P. J., Mlodzianowski, A. E., Meyers, B. S., Greenberg, R. L., and Bruce, M. L. 2006. *Transition to Home Care: Quality of Mental Health, Pharmacy, and Medical History Information.* Http://Dx.Doi.Org/10.2190/6N5P-5CXH-L750-A8HV 36 (3): 339–49. https://doi.org/10.2190/6N5P-5CXH-L750-A8HV.

Brunetto, Y., Farr-Wharton, R., and Shacklock, K. 2011. *Using the Harvard HRM Model to Conceptualise the Impact of Changes to Supervision upon HRM Outcomes for Different Types of Australian Public Sector Employees.* Https://Doi.Org/10.1080/09585192.2011.543633 22 (3): 553–73. https://doi.org/10.1080/09585192.2011.543633.

Calciolari, S., Cantu, E., and Fattore, G. 2011. "Performance Management and Goal Ambiguity: Managerial Implications in a Single Payer System." *Health Care Management Review* 36 (2): 164–74.

Calhoun, J. G., Rowney, R., Eng, E., and Hoffman, Y. 2016. Competency *Mapping and Analysis for Public Health Preparedness Training*

Initiatives Http://Dx.Doi.Org/10.1177/00333549051200S117 120 (SUPLL. 1): 91–99. https://doi.org/10.1177/00333549051200S117.

Camberlin, C., Senn, A., Leys, M., and De Laet, C., 2021. *Robot-Assisted Surgery: Health Technology Assessment KCE Reports 104C.* Accessed September 10, 2021. http://www.kce.fgov.be.

Cardinaels, E., Roodhooft, F., and Van Herck, G. 2004. "Drivers of Cost System Development in Hospitals: Results of a Survey." *Health Policy* 69 (2): 239–52. https://doi.org/10.1016/j.healthpol.2004.04.009.

Carini, E., Gabutti, I., Frisicale, E. M., Di Pilla, A., Pezzullo, A. M., de Waure, C., Cicchetti, A., Boccia, S., and Specchia, M. L. 2020. "Assessing Hospital Performance Indicators. What Dimensions? Evidence from an Umbrella Review." *BMC Health Services Research* 20 (1): 1–13. https://doi.org/10.1186/s12913-020-05879-y.

Cash-Gibson, L., Tigova, O., Alonso, A., Binkley, G., and Rosenmöller, M. 2019. "Project Integrate: Developing a Framework to Guide Design, Implementation and Evaluation of People-Centred Integrated Care Processes." *International Journal of Integrated Care* 19 (1): 1–11. https://doi.org/10.5334/ijic.4178.

Cavalleri, M., Morstabilini, R., and Reni, G. 2005. "Integrating Telemonitoring with Clinical Information Systems: A Case Study." *Annual International Conference of the IEEE Engineering in Medicine and Biology - Proceedings* 7 VOLS: 573–76. https://doi.org/10.1109/IEMBS.2005.1616477.

Cicchetti, A. 2019. Impact HTA, research presentation. Catholic University of Rome, Italy. Unpublished presentation.

Cresswell, K., and Sheikh, A. 2013. "Organizational Issues in the Implementation and Adoption of Health Information Technology Innovations: An Interpretative Review." *International Journal of Medical Informatics* 82 (5). https://doi.org/10.1016/J.IJMEDINF.2012.10.007.

Debono, D., Taylor, N., Lipworth, W., Greenfield, D., Travaglia, J., Black, D., and Braithwaite, J. 2017. "Applying the Theoretical Domains Framework to Identify Barriers and Targeted Interventions to Enhance Nurses' Use of Electronic Medication Management Systems in Two Australian Hospitals." *Implementation Science : IS* 12 (1). https://doi.org/10.1186/S13012-017-0572-1.

Definition of Clinical Data Repository (CDR) - *Gartner Information Technology Glossary.* 2021. Accessed September 10, 2021. https://www.gartner.com/en/information-technology/glossary/cdr-clinical-data-repository.

Dharampal, N., Cameron, C., Dixon, E., Ghali, W., and Quan, M.L. 2016. "Attitudes and Beliefs about the Surgical Safety Checklist: Just Another Tick Box?" *Canadian Journal of Surgery. Journal Canadien de Chirurgie* 59 (4): 268–75. https://doi.org/10.1503/CJS.002016.

Douglas, S., Hood, C., Overmans, T., and Scheepers, F. 2019. "Gaming the System: Building an Online Management Game to Spread and Gather Insights into the Dynamics of Performance Management Systems*." *Public Management Review* 21 (10): 1560–76. https://doi.org/10.1080/14719037.2019.1571277.

Elliott, A. F., Davidson, A., Lum, F., Chiang, M. F., Saaddine, J. B., Zhang, X., Crews, J. E., and Chou, C. F. 2012. "Use of Electronic Health Records and Administrative Data for Public Health Surveillance of Eye Health and Vision-Related Conditions in the United States." *American Journal of Ophthalmology* 154 (6): S63–70. https://doi.org/10.1016/J.AJO.2011.10.002.

Englebright, J., Aldrich, K., and Taylor, C.R. 2014. "Defining and Incorporating Basic Nursing Care Actions Into the Electronic Health Record." *Journal of Nursing Scholarship* 46 (1): 50–57. https://doi.org/10.1111/JNU.12057.

Esmaeilzadeh, P., Sambasivan, M., Kumar, N., and Nezakhati, H. 2011. "Adoption of Technology Applications in Healthcare: The Influence of Attitude toward Knowledge Sharing on Technology Acceptance in a Hospital." *International Conference on U- and E-Service, Science and Technology.*

Essex, B., Doig, R., Rosenthal, J., and Doherty, J. 1991. "The Psychiatric Discharge Summary: A Tool for Management and Audit." *British Journal of General Practice* 41 (349).

Fanelli, S., Lanza, G., and Zangrandi, A. 2018. "Competences Management for Improving Performance in Health Organizations: The Niguarda Hospital in Milan." *International Journal of Health Care Quality Assurance* 31 (4): 337–49. https://doi.org/10.1108/IJHCQA-02-2017-0035.

Ferrara, F. 2020. Lessons in ICT applied to the healthcare sector. Catholic University of Rome, Italy. Unpublished presentation.

FIASO (Italian Federation of Hospitals and Healthcare Organizations). 2021. *Managing Competencies of Middle Management in the Italian National Health Service (Gestione, Sviluppo E Valorizzazione Delle Competenze Del Middle Management Del SSN)*. Egea.

Gabutti, I. 2019. "Hiring the Right CEO: A Pilot Explorative Study of the Most Innovative CEOs' Career Pathways in the Healthcare Sector." *International Journal of Healthcare Management*. https://doi.org/10.1080/20479700.2018.1562613.

Gabutti, I., Mascia, D., and Cicchetti, A. 2017. "Exploring 'Patient-Centered' Hospitals: A Systematic Review to Understand Change." *BMC Health Services Research* 17 (1). https://doi.org/10.1186/s12913-017-2306-0.

Gabutti, I., and Cicchetti, A. 2017. "Translating Strategy into Practice: A Tool to Understand Organizational Change in a Spanish University Hospital. An in-Depth Analysis in Hospital Clinic." *International Journal of Healthcare Management* 13 (2): 142–55. https://doi.org/10.1080/20479700.2017.1336837.

Gagnon, M.P., Desmartis, M., Labrecque, M., Car, J., Pagliari, C., Pluye, P., Frémont, P., Gagnon, J., Tremblay, N., and Légaré, F. 2012. "Systematic Review of Factors Influencing the Adoption of Information and Communication Technologies by Healthcare Professionals." *Journal of Medical Systems* 36 (1): 241–77. https://doi.org/10.1007/S10916-010-9473-4.

Gao, T., and Gurd, B. 2015. "Meeting the Challenge in Performance Management: The Diffusion and Implementation of the Balanced Scorecard in Chinese Hospitals." *Health Policy and Planning* 30 (2): 234–41. https://doi.org/10.1093/heapol/czu008.

Garavand, A., Mohseni, M., Asadi, H., Etemadi, M., Moradi-Joo, M., and Moosavi, A. 2016. "Factors Influencing the Adoption of Health Information Technologies: A Systematic Review." *Electronic Physician* 8 (8): 2713. https://doi.org/10.19082/2713.

Giacomelli, G. 2019. "The Role of Hybrid Professionals in the Public Sector: A Review and Research Synthesis." *Https://Doi.Org/10.1080/14719037.2019.1642952* 22 (11): 1624–51. https://doi.org/10.1080/14719037.2019.1642952.

Gile, P. P., Buljac-Samardzic, M., and Van De Klundert, J. 2018. "The Effect of Human Resource Management on Performance in Hospitals in Sub-Saharan Africa: A Systematic Literature Review." *Human Resources for Health 2018 16:1* 16 (1): 1–21. https://doi.org/10.1186/S12960-018-0298-4.

Giordanengo, A., Bradway, M., Pedersen, R., Grøttland, A., Hartvigsen, G., and Årsand, E. 2016. "Integrating Data from Apps, Wearables and Personal Electronic Health Record (PEHR) Systems with Clinicians' Electronic Health Records (EHR) Systems." *International Journal of Integrated Care* 16 (5): 16. https://doi.org/10.5334/IJIC.2565.

Grossi, A., Hoxhaj, I., Gabutti, I., Carini, E., Pezzullo, A. M., Cacciatore, P., Specchia, M.L., Cicchetti, A., Boccia, S., and de Waure, C. 2019. "Hospital Contextual Factors Affecting the Use of Health Technologies: A Systematic Review." *European Journal of Public Health* 29 (Supplement_4): 1–12. https://doi.org/10.1093/eurpub/ckz186.302.

Hallberg, D., and Salimi, N. 2020. "Qualitative and Quantitative Analysis of Definitions of E-Health and m-Health." *Healthcare Informatics Research* 26 (2): 119–28. https://doi.org/10.4258/HIR.2020.26.2.119.

Halmesmäki, E., Pasternack, I., and Roine, R. 2016. "Hospital-Based Health Technology Assessment (HTA) in Finland: A Case Study on Collaboration between Hospitals and the National HTA Unit." *Health Research Policy and Systems* 14 (1): 2–9. https://doi.org/10.1186/s12961-016-0095-2.

Heerema-Poelman, A., Stuive, I., and Wempe, J. B. 2013. "Adherence to a Maintenance Exercise Program 1 Year after Pulmonary Rehabilitation: What Are the Predictors of Dropout?" *Journal of Cardiopulmonary Rehabilitation and Prevention* 33 (6): 419–26. https://doi.org/10.1097/HCR.0B013E3182A5274A.

Holt, D. H., Rod, M. H., Waldorff, S. B., and Tjørnhøj-Thomsen, T. 2018. "Elusive Implementation: An Ethnographic Study of Intersectoral Policymaking for Health." *BMC Health Services Research* 18 (1): 1–12. https://doi.org/10.1186/s12913-018-2864-9.

Hurlen, P., Østbye, T., Borthne, A. S., and Gulbrandsen, P. 2010. "Does Improved Access to Diagnostic Imaging Results Reduce Hospital Length of Stay? A Retrospective Study." *BMC Health Services Research 2010 10:1* 10 (1): 1–5. https://doi.org/10.1186/1472-6963-10-262.

Ileri, Y., and Arik, O. 2018. "Investigation of Resistance, Perception and Attitudes of Employees against Change in Information Systems Using Change Management Approach: A Study in a University Hospital." *Journal of Information & Knowledge Management* 17 (4).

IMPACT HTA, 2021. https://www.impact-hta.eu/ Accessed September 13, 2021.

Keel, G., Muhammad, R., Savage, C., Spaak, J., Gonzalez, I., Lindgren, P., Guttmann, C., and Mazzocato, P. 2020. "Time-Driven Activity-Based Costing for Patients with Multiple Chronic Conditions: A Mixed-Method Study to Cost Care in a Multidisciplinary and Integrated Care Delivery Centre at a University-Affiliated Tertiary Teaching Hospital in Stockholm, Sweden." *BMJ Open* 10 (6): e032573. https://doi.org/10.1136/bmjopen-2019-032573.

Keel, G., Savage, C., Muhammad, R., and Mazzocato, P. 2017. "Time-Driven Activity-Based Costing in Health Care: A Systematic Review of the Literature." *Health Policy* 121 (7): 755–63. https://doi.org/10.1016/j.healthpol.2017.04.013.

Kellner, A., Townsend, K., Wilkinson, A., Lawrence, S. A., and Greenfield, D. 2016. "Learning to Manage: Development Experiences of Hospital Frontline Managers." *Human Resource*

Management Journal 26 (4): 505–22. https://doi.org/10.1111/1748-8583.12119.

Kriegel, J., Tuttle-Weidinger, L., Schiefer, L., and Schwarz, S. 2019. "Management of Support Processes in Austrian Hospitals: Integrated Network of Primary Care Processes and Support Processes." *International Journal of Healthcare Management* 12 (2).

Kringos, D. S., Sunol, R., Wagner, C., Mannion, R., Michel, P., Klazinga, N. S., and Groene, O. 2015. "The Influence of Context on the Effectiveness of Hospital Quality Improvement Strategies: A Review of Systematic Reviews Quality, Performance, Safety and Outcomes." *BMC Health Services Research* 15 (1). https://doi.org/10.1186/s12913-015-0906-0.

Kristensen, N., Nymann, C., and Konradsen, H. 2016. "Implementing Research Results in Clinical Practice- the Experiences of Healthcare Professionals." *BMC Health Services Research* 16 (1): 1–10. https://doi.org/10.1186/s12913-016-1292-y.

Krupička, J. 2021. "The Performance Management Design in Public Hospitals: A Case Study." *NISPAcee Journal of Public Administration and Policy* 14 (1): 107–33. https://doi.org/10.2478/nispa-2021-0005.

Kurunmaki, L. 1999. "Professional vs Financial Capital in the Field of Health Care. Struggles for the Redistribution of Power and Control." *Accounting, Organizations and Society* 24 (2): 95–124. https://econpapers.repec.org/RePEc:eee:aosoci:v:24:y:1999:i:2:p:95-124.

Langer, M., Castellari, R., Locatelli, P., Sini, E., Torresani, M., Facchini, R. and Moser, R. 2014. "An Integrated Approach to Safety-Driven and ICT-Enabled Process Reengineering: Methodological Advice and a Case Study." *Studies in Health Technology and Informatics* 201: 203–10. https://doi.org/10.3233/978-1-61499-415-2-203.

Lee, H. W., Ramayah, T., and Zakaria, N. 2011. "External Factors in Hospital Information System (HIS) Adoption Model: A Case on Malaysia." *Journal of Medical Systems 2011 36:4* 36 (4): 2129–40. https://doi.org/10.1007/S10916-011-9675-4.

Lee, O. F., and Guster, D. 2012. "Virtualized Disaster Recovery Model for Large Scale Hospital and Healthcare Systems." *Advancing Technologies and Intelligence in Healthcare and Clinical Environments Breakthroughs*, June, 307–19. https://doi.org/10.4018/978-1-4666-1755-1.CH022.

Lega, F., and De Pietro, C. 2005. "Converging Patterns in Hospital Organization: Beyond the Professional Bureaucracy." *Health Policy (Amsterdam, Netherlands)* 74 (3): 261–81. https://doi.org/10.1016/J.HEALTHPOL.2005.01.010.

Lega, F., Longo, F., and Rotolo, A. 2013. "Decoupling the Use and Meaning of Strategic Plans in Public Healthcare." *BMC Health Services Research* 13 (1): 1–11. https://doi.org/10.1186/1472-6963-13-5.

Leung, L., and Chen, C. 2019. "E-Health/m-Health Adoption and Lifestyle Improvements: Exploring the Roles of Technology Readiness, the Expectation-Confirmation Model, and Health-Related Information Activities." *Telecommunications Policy* 43 (6): 563–75. https://doi.org/10.1016/J.TELPOL.2019.01.005.

Lievens, F., Sanchez, J.I. and de Corte, W. 2004. "Easing the Inferential Leap in Competency Modelling: The Effects of Task-Related Information and Subject Matter Expertise." *Personnel Psychology* 57 (4): 881–904. https://doi.org/10.1111/J.1744-6570.2004.00009.X.

Ling, T., Bardsley, M., Adams, J., Lewis, R., and Roland, M. 2010. "Evaluation of UK Integrated Care Pilots: Research Protocol." *International Journal of Integrated Care* 10 (3): 1–15. https://doi.org/10.5334/ijic.513.

Locatelli, P., Restifo, N., Gastaldi, L., Sini, E., and Torresani, M. 2010. "The Evolution of Hospital Information Systems and the Role of Electronic Patient Records: From the Italian Scenario to a Real Case." *Studies in Health Technology and Informatics* 160 (PART 1): 247–51. https://doi.org/10.3233/978-1-60750-588-4-247.

Mannion, R., and Braithwaite, J.. 2012. "Unintended Consequences of Performance Measurement in Healthcare: 20 Salutary Lessons from the English National Health Service." *Internal Medicine Journal* 42 (5): 569–74. https://doi.org/10.1111/j.1445-5994.2012.02766.x.

McClelland, D. C. 1973. "Testing for competence rather than for intelligence." *American Psychologist*, 28(1), 1–14. https://doi.org/10.1037/h0034092."

Melnick, E. R., Sinsky, C. A., Dyrbye, L. N., Trockel, M., West, C. P., Nedelec, L., and Shanafelt, T. 2020. "Association of Perceived Electronic Health Record Usability With Patient Interactions and Work-Life Integration Among US Physicians." *JAMA Network Open* 3 (6): e207374–e207374. https://doi.org/10.1001/JAMANETWORKOPEN.2020.7374.

Miller, A., Koola, J. D., Matheny, M. E., Ducom, J. H., Slagle, J. M., Groessl, E. J., Minter, F. F., Garvin, J. H., Weinger, M. B. and Ho, S. B. 2018. "Application of Contextual Design Methods to Inform Targeted Clinical Decision Support Interventions in Sub-Specialty Care Environments." *International Journal of Medical Informatics* 117 (September): 55–65. https://doi.org/10.1016/J.IJMEDINF.2018.05.005.

Mitchell, L., and Boak, G. 2009. "Developing Competence Frameworks in UK Healthcare: Lessons from Practice." *Journal of European Industrial Training*, Vol. 33 No. 8/9, pp. 701-717. https://doi.org/10.1108/03090590910993580.

Muijen, M., Marks, I., Connolly, J., and Audini, B. 1992. "Home Based Care and Standard Hospital Care for Patients with Severe Mental Illness: A Randomised Controlled Trial." *British Medical Journal* 304 (6829): 749–54. https://doi.org/10.1136/BMJ.304.6829.749.

Munn, S. R. 2014. "Hospital-Based Health Technology Assessment: Insights from New Zealand." *PharmacoEconomics* 32 (9): 815–17. https://doi.org/10.1007/s40273-014-0202-6.

Nanji, K. C., Cina, J., Patel, N., Churchill, W., Gandhi, T. K., and Poon, E. G. 2009. "Overcoming Barriers to the Implementation of a Pharmacy Bar Code Scanning System for Medication Dispensing: A Case Study." *Journal of the American Medical Informatics*

Association: *JAMIA* 16 (5): 645–50. https://doi.org/10.1197/JAMIA.M3107.

Norrish, B., and Rundall, T. 2001. "Hospital Restructuring and the Work of Registered Nurses." *Milbank Q.* 79 (1): 55–79.

Ogrinc, G., Davies, L., Goodman, D., Batalden, P., Davidoff, F., and Stevens, D. 2016. "SQUIRE 2.0 (Standards for QUality Improvement Reporting Excellence): Revised Publication Guidelines from a Detailed Consensus Process." *BMJ Quality & Safety* 25 (12): 986–92. https://doi.org/10.1136/BMJQS-2015-004411.

Ortaköylü, M. G., Altın, S., Bahadır, A., Ürer, H.N., Koşar, F., and Coskun, A. 2016. "Activity-Based Costing Management and Hospital Cost in Patients with Chronic Obstructive Pulmonary Disease." *Electronic Journal of General Medicine* 13 (2): 116–26. https://doi.org/10.15197/ejgm.1537.

Park, H. A., Cho, I., and Chung, E. 2011. "Exploring Use of a Clinical Data Repository Containing International Classification for Nursing Practice-Based Nursing Practice Data." *CIN - Computers Informatics Nursing* 29 (7): 419–26. https://doi.org/10.1097/NCN.0B013E3181F9DC6E.

Parsons, R., Gustafson, G., Murray, P., Dwore, R., Smith, P., and Vorderer, L. 1997. "Hospital Administrators' Career Paths: Which Way to the Top." *Health Care Management Review* 22 (4): 82–92.

Rosemond, C. A., Hanson, L. C., Ennett, S. T., Schenck, A. P., and Weiner, B. J. 2012. "Implementing Person-Centered Care in Nursing Homes." *Health Care Management Review* 37 (3): 257–66. https://doi.org/10.1097/HMR.0B013E318235ED17.

Ruef, M., and Scott, R. 1998. "A Multidimensional Model of Organizational Legitimacy: Hospital Survival in Changing Institutional Environments." *Administrative Science Quarterly* 43 (4): 877–904.

Sacco, P 2019. Lessons of Managerial Accounting. *Catholic University of Milan, Italy. Unpublished presentation.*

Schnoor, J., Braehler, E., and Heyde, C.-E. 2019. "Did We Learn the Lesson after 60 Years of Management by Objectives? A Survey among Former Physician Executives in German Hospitals." *Work* 62 (2): 353–59. https://doi.org/10.3233/WOR-192869.

Scott, R., Ruef, M., Mendel, P. J., and Caronna, C. A. 2000. *"Institutional Change and Healthcare Organizations." From Professional Dominance to Managed Care*. University of Chicago Press: Chicago.

Seto, E., Morita, P. P., Tomkun, J., Lee, T. M., Ross, H., Reid-Haughian, C., Kaboff, A., Mulholland, D., and Cafazzo, J. A. 2019. "Implementation of a Heart Failure Telemonitoring System in Home Care Nursing: Feasibility Study." *JMIR Med Inform 2019;7(3):E11722* https://Medinform.Jmir.Org/2019/3/E11722 7 (3): e11722. https://doi.org/10.2196/11722.

Shipton, H., Sanders, K., Atkinson, C., and Frenkel, S. 2016. "Sense-Giving in Health Care: The Relationship between the HR Roles of Line Managers and Employee Commitment." *Human Resource Management Journal* 26 (1): 29–45. https://doi.org/10.1111/1748-8583.12087.

Smith, M., Lix, L. M., Azimaee, M., Enns, J. E., Orr, J., Hong, S., and Roos, L. L. 2018. "Assessing the Quality of Administrative Data for Research: A Framework from the Manitoba Centre for Health Policy." *Journal of the American Medical Informatics Association* 25 (3): 224–29. https://doi.org/10.1093/JAMIA/OCX078.

Steele Gray, C., Barnsley, J., Gagnon, D., Belzile, L., Kenealy, T., Shaw, J., Sheridan, N., Wankah Nji, and Wodchis, W. P. 2018. "Using Information Communication Technology in Models of Integrated Community-Based Primary Health Care: Learning from the ICOACH Case Studies." *Implementation Science* 13 (1): 1–14. https://doi.org/10.1186/s13012-018-0780-3.

Struik, M. H., Koster, F., Schuit, A. J., Nugteren, R., Veldwijk, J., and Lambooij, M. S. 2014. "The Preferences of Users of Electronic Medical Records in Hospitals: Quantifying the Relative Importance of Barriers and Facilitators of an Innovation." *Implementation Science 2014 9:1* 9 (1): 1–11. https://doi.org/10.1186/1748-5908-9-69.

Szydlowski, S., and Smith, C. 2009. "Perspectives from Nurse Leaders and Chief Information Officers on Health Information Technology Implementation." *Hospital Topics* 87 (1): 3–9. https://doi.org/10.3200/HTPS.87.1.3-9.

Trebble, T.M., Heyworth, N., Clarke, N., Powell, T., and Hockey, P.M. 2014. "Managing Hospital Doctors and Their Practice: What Can We Learn about Human Resource Management from Non-Healthcare Organisations?" *BMC Health Services Research* 14 (1): 1–11. https://doi.org/10.1186/s12913-014-0566-5.

Tunc, T., and Kutanis, R. O. 2009. "Role Conflict, Role Ambiguity, and Burnout in Nurses and Physicians at a University Hospital in Turkey." *Nursing & Health Sciences* 11 (4): 410–16. https://doi.org/10.1111/J.1442-2018.2009.00475.X.

Udlis, K. A., and Mancuso, J. M. 2015. "Perceptions of the Role of the Doctor of Nursing Practice-Prepared Nurse: Clarity or Confusion." *Journal of Professional Nursing* 31 (4): 274–83. https://doi.org/10.1016/J.PROFNURS.2015.01.004.

Varabyova, Y., Blankart, C. R., Greer, A. L., and Schreyögg, J. 2017. "The Determinants of Medical Technology Adoption in Different Decisional Systems: A Systematic Literature Review." *Health Policy (Amsterdam, Netherlands)* 121 (3): 230–42. https://doi.org/10.1016/J.HEALTHPOL.2017.01.005.Varonen, H., Kortteisto, T., and Kaila, M. 2008. "What May Help or Hinder the Implementation of Computerized Decision Support Systems (CDSSs): A Focus Group Study with Physicians." *Family Practice* 25 (3): 162–67. https://doi.org/10.1093/FAMPRA/CMN020.

Vina, E. R., Rhew, D. C., Weingarten, S. R., Weingarten, J. B., and Chang, J. T. 2009. "Relationship between Organizational Factors and Performance among Pay-for-Performance Hospitals." *Journal of General Internal Medicine* 24 (7): 833–40. https://doi.org/10.1007/s11606-009-0997-6.

Vukovic, V., Favaretti, C., Ricciardi, W. and de Waure, C. 2018. "Health Technology Assessment Evidence on e-Health/m-Health Technologies: Evaluating the Transparency and Thoroughness." *International Journal of Technology Assessment in Health Care* 34 (1): 87–96. https://doi.org/10.1017/S0266462317004512.

WHO/Europe | *Health Technologies and Medicines - Health Technology Assessment.* n.d. Accessed September 10, 2021. https://www.euro.who.int/en/health-topics/Health-systems/health-technologies-and-medicines/policy-areas/health-technology-assessment.

Chapter 4

MEASURING HOSPITAL PERFORMANCE

ABSTRACT

All the managerial interventions hospitals may carry out are aimed at reaching top "hospital performance". Nevertheless, this is an articulated concept that must be interpreted from a multi-dimensional point of view. The risk is that of privileging some dimensions of performance at the risk of others. Typically, it is frequent to focus on short-term objectives rather than on long-term (and shared) ones. However, this approach is in contrast with hospitals' main mission which is that of "producing healthy people". This objective can be explained through the concept of "value."

Keywords: hospital performance, performance dimensions, value

4.1. INTRODUCTION

Any strategic plan at the hospital level must necessarily be oriented towards the achievement of key hospital goals. Indeed, the assessment of the set of managerial interventions holds exactly on their ability of (contributing to) reaching the desired hospital performance. In a way, defining the latter clearly, is the only way to enable the whole organization to understand "where the hospital is going". Nevertheless, defining this strategic orientation is challenging. The mere concept of hospital performance is ambiguous and subject to various interpretations by different stakeholders. This is why a solid, structured, balanced and fair definition of hospitals' objectives is the starting point of any managerial team. Any form of ambiguity in the definition of these objectives is likely to cause multiple issues across the entire hospital.

4.2. Understanding the Dimensions of Hospital Performance

It is widely recognized that assessing the performance of hospitals takes into account multiple aspects and dimensions. This is in part due to the organizational and procedural complexity of such entities and to the high number of stakeholders involved in their activities. Each of these is likely to have specific priorities as well as interpretations of the expression "hospital performance". Patients, professionals (and different categories of these), policy makers, external associations, payors are all examples of actors that are likely to have different views on what exactly should be intended by hospital performance. Moreover, personal values, cultures, or even the specific instant in which one is called to express an opinion, are also likely to affect individual or category priorities. Therefore, it is still difficult to assess performance of hospitals concretely. The task is even more challenging if we consider the differences in the main characteristics of hospitals (e.g., dimension, ownership, degree of clinical focus, geographical location).

Nevertheless, it is possible to think of hospital performance as the sum of various dimensions, each of which contributes to a more general concept of success. These dimensions must of course be balanced and integrated in systematic ways, so not to frustrate any of them. A recent study (Carini et al. 2020) has investigated the various dimensions that make up hospital performance, providing a common language to identify, frame and address performance assessment. Table 5 summarizes the main dimensions detected in this study.

Table 5. The dimensions of hospital performance

Dimension	Description
Efficiency	This dimension can be defined as the optimal allocation of available healthcare resources that maximize health outcomes for society ("HtaGlossary.Net | Efficiency" 2021). Similarly, it can be referred to as the hospital's optimal use of inputs to yield maximal outputs, given the available resources (Veillard et al. 2005).
Clinical effectiveness	This dimension has to do with the appropriateness and competence which allows to deliver clinical care and services with the maximum benefit for all patients (Veillard et al. 2005). This dimension can be further divided in appropriateness of care, conformity of processes of care, and outcomes of care and safety processes. Indicators include rates of mortality, of readmission, and of survival (Simou et al. 2014).
Safety	This dimension is referred both to patients and professionals in terms of the ability to avoid, prevent and reduce harmful interventions or risks. It is related both to the safety of people and of the environment (Veillard et al. 2005; Simou et al. 2014).
Timeliness	This dimension is referred to the time needed to be addressed to specific treatments (Simou et al. 2014).
Responsive governance	This dimension can be thought of as the degree of responsiveness to community needs, to ensure care continuity and coordination, to promote health and provide care to all citizens (Veillard et al. 2005).
Staff orientation	This dimension is defined in terms of recognition of professionals' individual needs, health promotion and safety initiatives, behavioral responses (Veillard et al. 2005). Indicators may assess absenteeism, working environment satisfaction, overtime working, burnout and continuous education.
Patient-centeredness	This dimension concerns a set of indicators which pay attention to patients' and families' orientations. The main aim is to evaluate whether patients are placed at the center of care and service delivery (Veillard et al. 2005) and may be intended both in reference to their satisfaction and, primarily, as the ability to provide assistance when needed by the patient, where it is needed.

Source: Carini et al. 2020.

These dimensions should not be seen as isolated monads but rather always connected to each other. For example, clinical effectiveness must be consistent with efficiency, providing effective care in a sustainable way in the long run. The lively debate on conflicts emerging between clinical professionals and managerial teams testifies the challenging need of combining the perspectives of these two roles (Rivers, Woodward, and Munchus 1997). Performing in terms of safety is strictly connected to clinical effectiveness. The capability of a hospital to preserve patients' good health is the other side of the coin in assuring clinical quality. Clearly, a hospital should not only intervene to improve patients' health, but it must do so in such a way as to avoid exposing them to potential sources of personal harm. Moreover, safety is also referred to staff, which is frequently directly exposed to numerous risks and requires a structured and solid organizational apparatus to preserve its health (Ancarani, Di Mauro, and Giammanco 2017). The dimension of patient-centeredness may be interpreted in a strictly interconnected way with that of responsive governance (Lega and De Pietro 2005). If, on the one hand, patient-centeredness may assume a 'double face', covering both the dimension of patient satisfaction as well as that of continuity of care, on the other, responsive governance seems related to the capability of hospitals to monitor performance in an integrated manner (within its units and throughout different settings). The latter topic surely needs a deeper focus in the years to come (Rathert, Wyrwich, and Boren 2012).

In accordance with epidemiological patterns of developed countries, with ageing populations and the spread of multi-pathological chronic conditions, it is crucial to shift the conception of performance from a setting-oriented to a multi setting-oriented approach. Hospitals are by now one of the steps in patients' clinical pathways and it is misleading to assess their contribution to their final status of health in a completely isolated way (Brown and Menec 2018). Although it is important to isolate the effects of a specific setting from the others, it makes little sense to think of performance as something that can be obtained without structured interconnections with the other settings of the system. In this sense, all the efforts in assessing the overall quality of clinical pathways are key in guaranteeing a truly effective and efficient system. Put in other terms, the dimensions of patient-centeredness, intended not only within the hospital's boundaries but rather as a contribution to broader pathways, is possibly a key dimension in the assessment of hospital performance. This holds more and more true, the more our healthcare systems shift towards horizontal, integrated organizational solutions.

Clearly, it is therefore important to adopt and implement managerial and evaluation tools that allow to "balance" the different facets of hospital performance. Although the existing tools are many in number and variety (Cicchetti 2002), a tool that adequately adopts this multi-faceted principle is the Balanced Scorecard (BSC) (Vesty and Brooks 2017; Cebeci 2018). This is done by calibrating the different dimensions of performance at stake when carrying out the activities of the organization, balancing them jointly. Traditionally, the domains of performance assessed through BSCs in the private industry (not in healthcare) include the financial one, processes, customer satisfaction, learning and growth. These can possibly be applied to the healthcare sector too.

Although it is at times frustrating to think of hospitals as entities oriented towards financial performance, the importance of this domain is straightforward. Not only is this true for private hospitals (or for hospitals operating in privately - driven healthcare systems), but also for public (or private) ones operating on behalf on national health care services. Although a hospital's mission is to produce health and not to make profits, its financial sustainability is a key aspect of its performance. Indeed, some national health services have imposed financial balance as a rule for the hospitals operating on their behalf (Makie et al. 2002; Michel et al. 2019).

Assessing processes is also of the utmost importance in at least two ways. In the first place in connection to processes in a strict sense. Their number within a hospital's daily activity is uncountable (Feibert, Andersen, and Jacobsen 2019). Processes are activated in carrying out a surgical activity, in administering a drug, in using a technology, in fostering a communication flow. The swift, efficient, and safe implementation of processes is key for overall hospital performance. Moreover, the term process can be intended in a broader sense. By process, we can actually intend clinical pathways (Lawal et al. 2019), i.e. the sequence of steps a patient has to face during his/her continuum of care (within a hospital, in this case, but the same holds true across settings). Indicators able to measure the weight of deviations from procedures (or from clinical pathways) as well as their time of implementation, give crucial information on the ability of the hospital to perform activities in an efficient and effective way.

Customers' (whether internal staff or external patients) satisfaction is a priority for hospitals. This holds true in reference to patients, who have the choice of whether to keep using the services of that hospital or not based on the overall quality of the services they perceive (Chen et al. 2020), as well as to staff, which has the power to decide where to work and how much effort to put in its work (Cai et al. 2016).

Finally, in the learning and growth perspective it is paramount to make sure that hospitals feed their set of competencies and of knowledge (Provvidenza et al. 2020). Indicators able to capture the quantity and quality of training activities or – in the case of university and research hospitals – the scientific contribution to the academic society, are examples of dimensions that would belong to this area.

It is frequent that the array of performance domains that hospitals must monitor and assess are more numerous than the ones just described for typical BSCs. These are likely to be extended based on the set of performance dimensions discussed above which, in turn, might be further extended. For example, a hospital may decide to include a strictly clinical domain, or a domain connected to its impact on the surrounding area. Other possible performance domains may indeed include patient accessibility, safety, efficiency, equity, appropriateness, patient-centeredness (Cicchetti 2002). Furthermore, depending on the characteristics and features of the hospital, each domain can be given a more or less relevant weight compared to the others (this is why this is a "balanced" approach). Overall, the number of indicators to track and assess in a hospital is possibly countless. It is clear, therefore, that defining hospital performance must take into consideration a range of indicators and dimensions, none of which should be overlooked and each of which should be balanced within the general assessment of performance. Section 3.9. provides a brief description of the main functioning of balanced scorecards.

4.3. IMPLEMENTING BALANCED SCORECARDS IN HOSPITALS

Balanced scorecards built upon the dimensions described above may be applied within hospitals at various levels. There may be "apical" balanced scorecards to assess the overall performance of hospitals, or these may be implemented at the level of an organizational unit, so as to assess their contribution to overall performance. Moreover, they can be used at the micro-level to monitor the performance of specific teams or even professionals.

Balanced scorecards are usually divided in performance dimensions. Each of these is further articulated into Key performance areas. These are more specific articulations of the broader dimension of performance. In turn, each key performance area is further divided into key performance indicators. These are emblematic indicators that enable an overall assessment of the extent to which key performance areas have been successfully met. Indicators must be *SMART* (Doran et al. 1981). This acronym stands for (Bours 2014):

- Specific: the indicator must be able to be translated into operational terms and made visible. While the outcome/result itself can be broad, the indicator should be narrow and focus on the 'who' and 'what' of the intervention.
- Measurable: The indicator clearly and directly relates to the outcome. It is described without ambiguities. Parties have a common understanding of the indicator.

- Achievable and Attributable: The indicator has the capacity to be counted, observed, analyzed, tested, or challenged. If one cannot measure an indicator, then progress cannot be determined.
- Relevant: An indicator should be a valid measure of the result/outcome and be linked through research and professional expertise. The best way to think about relevance is to ensure that there is a relationship between what the indicator measures and the final performance of the organization.
- Timely: Indicators must be timely in several aspects. First, they must be timely in terms of the time spent in data collection. This relates to the resources that are available - staff and partner time being critical. Second, indicators must reflect the timing of collection. Finally, the time-lag between output delivery and the expected change in outcome and impact indicators must also be reflected in the indicators that are chosen.

Finally, each key performance area is assigned with a percentage weight which "balances" the various dimensions of performance according to their relevance referred to the unit or professional that is being assessed. This allows for fair evaluations that are not biased by situations in which units or professionals are not fully accountable over specific outcomes. Table 6 shows an example of a balanced scorecard of a hospital clinical directorate.

Alongside the challenges of measuring, monitoring, and affecting numerous dimensions of performance, hospitals face a further and extremely arduous one. As a matter of fact, this has to do with understanding their ultimate goal, which is not being efficient, patient-centered or innovative, but rather that of "producing healthy people".

As a matter of fact, hospital performance could be thought of as the ability of "producing value" within patients' continuum of care. The term "value", here, is ascribable to Porter's definition, which is "the patient health outcomes achieved per dollar spent". As stated by Porter, "value encompasses many of the other goals already embraced in healthcare, such as quality, safety, patient-centeredness, and cost containment, and integrates them. It is also fundamental to achieving other important goals such as improving equity and expanding access at reasonable cost" (Porter 2010).

Table 6. An example of a balanced scorecard of a clinical directorate of a hospital

Area of Performance	Key performance area (examples)	Key performance indicator (examples)	Balanced weight
Financial perspective	Cost containment	Mean cost per patient (yearly)	15%
		Expenditure for drugs (yearly)	
	Volumes of activities performed	% interventions cancelled (yearly)	15%
		Surgical procedures carried out/ surgical procedures planned (yearly)	
Customer perspective	Patients' satisfaction	% patients with positive satisfactions from questionnaire (yearly)	20%
		Number of formal complaints (yearly)	
	Staff's satisfaction	Rate of absenteeism (yearly)	5%
		Turnover rate (yearly)	
Internal processes perspective	Implementation of clinical pathways	Mean throughput time (yearly)	30%
		Patients treated through clinical pathways/ total patients admitted (yearly)	
Learning and growth perspective	Training activities	Hours of training provided to staff (yearly)	10%
		% of staff involved in non-mandatory training activities (yearly)	
	Scientific development	Number of publications (yearly)	5%
		Number of citation (yearly)	
			100%

Source: Author's elaboration.

Following this reasoning, there emerges an incredible misalignment across countries between what is measured concretely by hospitals and what is truly relevant to patients. The bias is probably due to the tendency of measuring what is easy to measure at the expense of the measurement of "health". If value is defined as patient health outcomes achieved relative to the costs of care (Porter 2010; Teng and Longworth 2013; Putera 2017), it is crucial to measure both health outcomes and costs not only in the short but also in the long run. In other terms, it is not possible to identify a single outcome that captures the results of care for a specific medical condition. On the contrary, one should assess a set of multidimensional outcomes that jointly constitute patient benefit, including survival, functional status, and sustainability of recovery. Cost, in the same vein, refers to the total costs involved in the full cycle of care for the medical condition (and not just to the costs involved during a specific episode of care) and include the full array of resources involved in caring for the patient, including inpatient, outpatient, and rehabilitative care, along with all associated drugs, devices, services, and ancillary equipment (Porter 2010; Garvelink and van der Nat 2019; Makdisse et al. 2020).

Accountability for value across the continuum of care should hence be shared among different professionals and providers who are involved in the treatment of patients at different stages of their clinical pathways. The problem arises insofar as providers (e.g., hospitals) tend to measure only the interventions they provide directly. This, in turn, produces incomplete and fragmented evaluations of the system's performance, usually failing to track outcomes over time such as sustainable recovery, need for ongoing interventions, or occurrences of treatment-induced illnesses. The use of the various types of indicators at the hospital level, therefore, is for sure fundamental but does not coincide with the measurement of outcomes. They should all be measured and monitored within a clear picture of how they affect real value in the (long-term) perspective of patients.

The effort of classifying and systematizing performance measurement techniques across hospitals is key at the organizational, regional/national, and possibly international levels. At the organizational level, the way in which performance is assessed is likely to have strong and direct effects on internal organizational and managerial equilibria, as well as on the implementation of the overall strategy of the hospital. Depending on the choice of 'key' performance dimensions, some units or directorates are likely to be held more or less performing. This, in turn, can affect internal equilibria due to, for example, prestige and allocation of resources (Maniadakis et al. 2008).

At the regional/national level this sort of assessment may have crucial effects on the access to resources. Not only in terms of monetary remunerations (due to patients' choice of being assisted in a certain hospital or to, as is the case in some healthcare systems, the decision of regions to finance more or less large amounts of clinical activities to a specific hospital), but also in terms of their appeal to professionals and industries of health technologies (Ghaferi , Osborne, and Dimick 2010).

At the international level, a common ground to assess performance would allow an indirect assessment of different healthcare systems. These are highly differentiated across countries and benchmarking efforts are frequently hindered by the lack of comparable data (Medin et al. 2013).

In this scenario, it is crucial to provide the basis for a possible common way of measuring hospital performance. Once this effort is carried out and spread throughout healthcare systems, hospitals are likely to develop a higher awareness on the effects of their organizational and managerial strategies. It is easier to play each instrument of the orchestra if the director has clear in mind what the final symphony should sound like.

CONCLUSION

All managerial interventions must be monitored and assessed based on their ability of pursuing the hospital's objectives. However, setting hospital objectives may be an arduous task in the first place. This is due not only to the number and complexity of the activities it carries out, but also to the different priorities of various professionals and stakeholders in general. In this scenario, it is important to include all the relevant dimensions of hospital performance in a balanced evaluation tool. Moreover, the evaluation of performance should hold on the "typical" indicators aimed at assessing the activities carried out *within* the hospital, but also on strategic forms of evaluation. The latter must explore the hospital's contribution to the success of broader activities and processes, such as the implementation of clinical pathways and the provision of integrated care.

REFERENCES

Ancarani, A., Di Mauro, C., and Giammanco, M. D. 2017. "Hospital Safety Climate and Safety Behavior: A Social Exchange Perspective." *Health Care Management Review* 42 (4): 341–51. https://doi.org/10.1097/HMR.0000000000000118.

Bours, Dennis. 2014. "A Good Start with S.M.A.R.T. (Indicators)." *Adaptation and Resilience M & E.*

Brown, C. L., and Menec, V. 2018. "Integrated Care Approaches Used for Transitions from Hospital to Community Care: A Scoping Review." *Canadian Journal on Aging / La Revue Canadienne Du Vieillissement* 37 (2): 145–70. https://doi.org/10.1017/S0714980818000065.

Cai, S., Cai, W., Deng, L., Cai, B., and Yu, M. 2016. "Hospital Organizational Environment and Staff Satisfaction in China: A Large-Scale Survey." *International Journal of Nursing Practice* 22 (6): 565–73. https://doi.org/10.1111/IJN.12471.

Carini, E., Gabutti, I., Frisicale, E.M., Di Pilla, A., Pezzullo, A.M., de Waure, C., Cicchetti, A., Boccia, S., and Specchia, M.L. 2020. "Assessing Hospital Performance Indicators. What Dimensions? Evidence from an Umbrella Review." *BMC Health Services Research* 20 (1): 1–13. https://doi.org/10.1186/s12913-020-05879-y

Cebeci, U. 2018. "Building Hospital Balanced Scorecard by Using Decision Support Approach." *IIOAB Journal* 9 (6): 42-47.

Chen, H., Cates, T., Taylor, M., and Cates, C. 2020. "Improving the US Hospital Reimbursement: How Patient Satisfaction in HCAHPS Reflects Lower Readmission." *International Journal of Health Care Quality Assurance* 33: 333–44.

Cicchetti, A. 2002. *The Organization of Hospitals (L'organizzazione dell'ospedale)*. Milano: Vita e Pensiero.

Feibert, D.C., Andersen, B., and Jacobsen, P. 2019. "Benchmarking Healthcare Logistics Processes: A Comparative Case Study of Danish and US Hospitals." *Total Quality Management & Business Excellence (Print Edition)* 30 (1–2): 108–34. https://doi.org/10.1080/14783363.2017.1299570.

Ghaferi, A.A., Osborne, N.H., and Dimick, J.B. 2010. "Does Voluntary Reporting Bias Hospital Quality Rankings?" *The Journal of Surgical Research* 161 (2): 190–94. https://doi.org/10.1016/J.JSS.2009.07.033.

Garvelink, M.M., and van der Nat, P.B. 2019. "Moving Forward with Value Based Healthcare: The Need for a Scientific Approach." *European Journal of Surgical Oncology* 45 (7): 1299. https://doi.org/10.1016/J.EJSO.2019.03.029.

HtaGlossary.Net | *Efficiency*. n.d. Accessed September 11, 2021. http://htaglossary.net/efficiency.

Lawal, Adegboyega K., Gary Groot, Donna Goodridge, Shannon Scott, and Leigh Kinsman. 2019. "Development of a Program Theory for Clinical Pathways in Hospitals: Protocol for a Realist Review." *Systematic Reviews 2019 8:1* 8 (1): 1–7. https://doi.org/10.1186/S13643-019-1046-0.

Lega F., and De Pietro, C. 2005. "Converging Patterns in Hospital Organization: Beyond the Professional Bureaucracy." *Health Policy (Amsterdam, Netherlands)* 74 (3): 261–81. https://doi.org/10.1016/J.HEALTHPOL.2005.01.010.

Makdisse, M., Ramos, P., Malheiro, D., Felix, M., Cypriano, A., Soares, J., Carneiro, A., Cendoroglo Neto, M., and Klajner, S. 2020. "What Do Doctors Think About Value-Based Healthcare? A Survey of Practicing Physicians in a Private Healthcare Provider in Brazil."

Value in Health Regional Issues 23 (December): 25–29. https://doi.org/10.1016/J.VHRI.2019.10.003.

Makie, T., Miyazaki, M., Kobayashi, S., Yamanaka, T., Kinukawa, N., Hanada, E., and Nose, Y. 2002. "A Simple Method for Calculating the Financial Balance of a Hospital, Based on Proportional Dividing." *Journal of Medical Systems 2002 26:2* 26 (2): 105–12. https://doi.org/10.1023/A:1014801808798.

Maniadakis, N., Kotsopoulos, N., Prezerakos, P., and Fantopoulos, J.Y. 2008. "Measuring Intra-Hospital Clinic Efficiency and Productivity: An Application to a Greek University General Hospital." *European Research Studies* XI.

Medin, E., Häkkinen, U., Linna, M., Anthun, K.S., Kittelsen S.A.C., and Rehnberg, C. 2013. "International Hospital Productivity Comparison: Experiences from the Nordic Countries." *Health Policy* 112 (1–2): 80–87. https://doi.org/10.1016/J.HEALTHPOL.2013.02.004.

Michel, M., Alberti, C., Carel, J.-C., and Chevreul, K. 2019. "Association of Pediatric Inpatient Socioeconomic Status With Hospital Efficiency and Financial Balance." *JAMA Network Open* 2 (10): e1913656–e1913656. https://doi.org/10.1001/JAMANETWORKOPEN.2019.13656.

Rivers, P.A., Woodard, B., and Munchus, G. 1997. "Organizational Power and Conflict Regarding the Hospital-Physician Relationship: Symbolic or Substantive?" *Health Services Management Research* 10 (2): 91–106. https://doi.org/10.1177/095148489701000110.

Porter, M.E. 2010. *What Is Value in Health Care?* Http://Dx.Doi.Org/10.1056/NEJMp1011024 363 (26): 2477–81. https://doi.org/10.1056/NEJMP1011024.

Provvidenza, C., Townley, A., Wincentak, J., Peacocke, S., and Kingsnorth, S. 2020. "Building Knowledge Translation Competency in a Community-Based Hospital: A Practice-Informed Curriculum for Healthcare Providers, Researchers, and Leadership." *Implementation Science 2020 15:1* 15 (1): 1–12. https://doi.org/10.1186/S13012-020-01013-Y.

Putera, I. 2017. "Redefining Health: Implication for Value-Based Healthcare Reform." *Cureus* 9 (3). https://doi.org/10.7759/CUREUS.1067.

Rathert, C., Wyrwich, M., and Boren, S. 2012. "Patient-Centered Care and Outcomes: A Systematic Review of the Literature." *Med Care Res Rev.* 70 (4): 351–79.

Simou, E., Pliatsika P., Koutsogeorgou, E., and Roumeliotou, A. 2014. "Developing a National Framework of Quality Indicators for Public Hospitals." *The International Journal of Health Planning and Management* 29 (3): e187–206. https://doi.org/10.1002/HPM.2237.

Teng, K.A., and Longworth, D.L. 2013. *Personalized Healthcare in the Era of Value-Based Healthcare.* Http://Dx.Doi.Org/10.2217/Pme.13.14 10 (3): 285–93. https://doi.org/10.2217/PME.13.14.

Veillard, J., Champagne, F., Klazinga, N., Kazandjian, V., Arah, O., and Guisset, A. 2005. "A Performance Assessment Framework for Hospitals: The WHO Regional Office for Europe PATH Project." *International Journal for Quality in Health Care : Journal of the International Society for Quality in Health Care* 17 (6): 487–96. https://doi.org/10.1093/INTQHC/MZI072.

Vesty, G., and Brooks, A. 2017. "St George Hospital: Flexible Budgeting, Volume Variance, and Balanced Scorecard Performance Measurement." *Issues in Accounting Education* 32 (3): 103–16. https://doi.org/10.2308/IACE-51588.

Chapter 5

SEIZING THE "ORCHESTRA'S SYMPHONY": DRIVING ALL MANAGERIAL TOOLS TOWARDS A COMMON GOAL

ABSTRACT

Managing a hospital successfully implies fostering overall coherence between its strategy and its managerial actions. Although obvious in principle, examples of discrepancies between hospital organizational charts and managerial tools are frequent, often leading to forms of decoupling from the intended effects of organizational models. Failing in linking in a clear way even only one managerial intervention to the hospital's strategy may lead to unsuccessful transformations. This may have costly consequences in financial and non-financial terms, both for the hospital and for society in general. Top management must lead the various units and all the professionals within hospitals towards common objectives and must clarify the role of each in reaching them.

Keywords: strategy implementation, managerial coherence, integrated approach

5.1. Introduction

One of the recurrent terms throughout this book is the word "integrated". Integration must occur, as discussed, *among* organizations given that they provide health services jointly. Integration, however, must also be pursued *within* hospitals, that are made up of numerous units and areas which must cooperate constantly. Integration, therefore, is not just an abstract term that describes cooperation between settings or units. Rather, it implies that managerial strategies too must be fully integrated. This holds true *within* hospitals, which must implement a coherent and target-oriented overall management strategy. This also holds true *across* organizations, that must gradually learn to operate in partnership with other actors. Rising the awareness of this challenge means changing rooted cultures that are bound to limit the potential of healthcare systems worldwide.

5.2. Driving Hospitals towards Performance Through an Integrated Approach

It is undoubted that managing a hospital is a challenging task. Although ever since the rise of new public management these organizations are adopting managerial approaches that are inspired by those of the private industry, hospitals are indeed different from typical private firms in many ways. This means that innovative managerial solutions must indeed be sought, in the awareness that both internal dynamics as well as the mere acceptation of what kind of results must be achieved, differ substantially from other sectors.

The starting point, therefore, is really to understand which results must be reached. The first main message here is that hospital performance is a multi-faceted concept that includes various dimensions (Carini et al. 2020). Each of them is important and must be assessed in an integrated and balanced way. Tools such as balanced scorecards, or other evaluation tools that provide an integrated perspective, are key in measuring and reaching "hospital performance". This would be difficult to achieve if not measured across its various acceptations. The second key message is that although we can think of hospital performance as the sum of many dimensions, each one of these must ultimately lead to a high performance in the hospital's concrete mission, which is that of "producing health". This idea, though, should not be intended as an achievement of the hospital on its own, but rather as a *contribution* to the joint action of a network of providers of care. Therefore, "traditional" forms of hospital evaluation must be somehow integrated with this vision of shared responsibility and accountability on overall performance. Concretely, this means that evaluation tools built on "typical" hospital performance indicators are in urgent need of being extended through the use of "shared" indicators. Moreover, exactly because of their balanced feature, new evaluation approaches can assign reasonable weights to shared indicators, so not to incur evaluations that are unjust or not adequate due to the concrete degree of accountability providers may have on certain dimensions of performance. Indeed, there still exist many reasons (e.g., reimbursement systems, organizational prestige, organizational accountability) that make it necessary to preserve forms of setting-specific evaluation (Dizdar et al. 2007; Dubas-Jakóbczyk and Koziel 2020). In general, though, the changing epidemiological features of the populations in developed countries make it difficult to think imagine that healthcare will remain effective and sustainable if not re-though in a patient-centered perspective (Capolongo et al. 2015; AlJaberi, Hussain, and Drake 2017; Gabutti, Mascia, and Cicchetti 2017; Maghsoudi, Cascón-Pereira, and Hernández Lara 2020).

At the hospital level, this means that these large and complex organizations must re-design their chart in a coherent way. If hospitals are to be thought of as "one of the links of the chain" (Güneş and Yaman 2017; Bravi et al. 2013; Di Vincenzo 2018), this means that their organizational charts must be such as to favor forms of *liaison* with the other members of this chain. New matrix-shaped organizational models which introduce and develop horizontal and transversal units in the hospital, are possibly the answer to this challenge (Cowen et al. 2008). Transversal units, which can be different in nature, usually assume two main connotations. On one hand they can be part of a progressive care approach and, though inside a hospital, they may be intended as the higher levels of intensity of care within the overall network of providers of care (Schneider and Pomidor 2014). On the other hand, transversal units may assume the configuration of clinical pathways, which "follow" patients across their continuum of care (Koval et al. 2004). It is easy to see how these units too are highly connected to primary health services and to other providers in general. Indeed, specific attention is needed not only in pursuing the general smoothness of pathways within the hospital, but rather it is paramount to manage effectively the "ties" before and after hospitalization, so as to pursue organizational smoothness across the *overall* pathway, intended as the patient's clinical journey across his/her lifespan (Hartgerink et al. 2014; Brown and Menec 2018; Liljas et al. 2019; Brown and Menec 2021).

To make this new organizational approach concrete, managers must make the whole organization converge towards this new configuration. This implies, in turn, updating all the managerial tools at their disposal in coherence with it. In other words, a transition from vertical to horizontal configurations cannot be carried out with the mere change of an organizational chart. The vast array of consolidated dynamics and behaviors must be accompanied towards change accordingly. Managerial accounting tools must be re-built around the new responsibility centers and the right balance between the accountability of these and of traditional units must be sought. As long as new units are not given resources and formal accountability for their actions, forms of resistance to change will arise. Yet, traditional units are still at the basis of hospital activity and should maintain their autonomy.

Most activities and processes in hospitals are scanned by health technologies. These have the power of affecting deeply how activities are carried out, but also need a deep understanding and acceptance by end-users if they are to be truly effective. When introducing or implementing health technologies, their impact and coherence with the hospital's configuration must be assessed and shared with end-users, so not to incur high investments that do not produce their intended effects.

A key topic in driving change in a hospital is setting up an effective information communication technology system. Horizontal and transversal approaches are bound to fail if they are not sustained by adequate strategies to store longitudinal data and to connect professionals and settings in time. This holds true *within* the hospital but also *across* settings, that are more and more in need of common databases to provide the best possible care to patients.

Finally, the set of human resource management tools must support new organizational configurations by updating the competencies present in key professional positions. This has implications on all the typical phases of human resource management and implies an update of the hospital's career pathways, so as to sustain the emerging role of new horizontal platforms and units.

5.3. AN EXAMPLE OF MANAGERIAL EFFECTIVENESS IN THE IMPLEMENTATION OF CHANGE: HAS HRM IMPLEMENTED THE CLINICAL DIRECTORATE MODEL EFFECTIVELY?

A recent study (Gabutti and Morandi 2018) has investigated the concrete degree of implementation of the clinical directorate model in Italian hospitals which were required to do so by law in the 90s. In particular, it has assessed how one of the managerial dimensions described in this book, i.e., human resource management, has contributed to its concrete implementation. Of course, any organizational transformation requires the *joint* support of *all* managerial tools and dimensions. Nevertheless, focusing on a specific dimension, may help understand its concrete "power" to support or hinder the intended change.

Literature suggests that beyond the HRM function, hospital middle managers too are responsible for implementing change through the use of

HRM tools (Herscovitch and Meyer 2002; Abrell-Vogel and Rowold 2014). Indeed, they are held capable of fostering employees' supportive behavior towards change, and their actions are thus finalized not only at influencing the adoption of change, but specially at driving its concrete implementation. This is because they can affect relevant processes, mechanisms and behaviors, also through the use of HRM tools within their organizational unit.

This study has investigated the adoption and degree of concrete implementation of relevant HRM practices at the clinical directorate level, holding on the assumption that to change organizations, it is necessary to change how people work and, therefore, the way of managing them. As mentioned, HRM covers various phases, among which selection and hiring, training and retention, evaluation, layoff. However, in the Italian public healthcare system, phases such as hiring and layoff are strongly regulated and leave little flexibility to managerial subjectivity. On the contrary, training and evaluation activities imply a high managerial autonomy. Therefore, the study has focused on clinical directors' impact on these two phases.

Training and retention tools have to do with fostering professional growth in terms of knowledge, skills and organizational behaviors; evaluation tools aim at assuring that the goals set are concretely achieved by people and teams. Specifically, the latter category can assume two different configurations: the first has to do with *controlling* the correct implementation of processes and procedures (due to the difficulty of measuring outputs and outcomes of healthcare processes, it is necessary to standardize them to reduce variability of results); the second has to do with a *management-by-objectives* perspective (i.e., the recognition of benefits and economic incentives related to the achievement of preconceived objectives).

In other words, the study held on the assumption that scenarios characterized by innovative and lively HRM systems have most likely been able to truly implement the clinical directorate model, avoiding the presence of decoupling phenomena and overcoming barriers and people's resistances to change.

In this vein, the study has investigated the extent to which HRM practices have permeated clinical directorates and their daily functioning in Italy. The sample was made up of 65 clinical directorates, belonging to 33 Italian health care organizations. Each healthcare organization autonomously selected two clinical directorates (except for one organization, in which only one was selected). Data were gathered through a national survey funded by the Italian Ministry of Health, within a broader project.

The survey consisted in 50 questions which focused on the implementation of HRM practices within clinical directorates and was addressed to clinical directors. It focused on the presence and concrete degree of application of three different types of human resource managerial practices: training-related, control-related, and objectives-related HRM tools.

To measure the degree of development of the three dimensions, the 50 items (questions) were divided into the three HRM families, based on their pertinence to each. In particular, for each category, not only was there an assessment of the mere presence or absence of the relevant specific practices, but also their *concrete degree of implementation* was investigated. To do so, questions not only measured statements about the "adoption" of a practice, but further explored their implementation through dimensions such as, for example, the frequency with which specific activities were carried out or the number of people involved in them. An example referred to an objectives-related tool can clarify the approach:

Question A277: Do you apply financial and/or nonfinancial incentives to the degree to which the clinical directorate's objectives are concretely reached?

- No
- Yes (please specify type of incentive)

Question A278: If present, to what sort of objectives are these incentives related?

- Assistance
- Research activities
- Teaching activities
- Containment of costs
- Other (please specify)

Results were then translated into scores by assigning a maximum theoretical absolute value to each question, translating them then into percentage scores. Following from the same example:

Question A277:

Answers No = 0; Answers yes = 1 (absolute score)
Answers No = 0%; Answers yes = 100% (percentage score)

Question A278:

No item is selected or mentioned = 0; 1 item = 1; 2 items = 2; ...
n items = n (absolute score)
No item is selected or mentioned = 0%; 1 item = 1/n%;
2 items = 2/n%;
n items = 100% (percentage score)

Table 7 shows the main contents at the basis of the questions ascribable to the three HRM practices' families, as well as the mean percentage implementation scores they reached within the sample (being often more than one item ascribable to such contents, the score indicated is the average one).

By translating the answers to the questions into a system of percentage scores, a mean percentage of implementation (with respect to a theoretical 100% implementation) in each clinical directorate, for each of the three families of tools was calculated. The degree to which Italian clinical directorates had concretely implemented the "ideal set" of HRM practices within their daily activities, in terms of scores reached compared to a theoretical maximum, are illustrated in Figures 18, 19 and 20.

Table 7. Contents of training-, control-, and objectives-related HRM tools and percentage implementation scores

Training tools	Score (%)	Control tools	Score (%)	Objectives tools	Score (%)
Training through practical experience (learning by doing)	87	Reports and documentation at clinical directorate level	89	Evaluation by objectives	92
Training Programs provided at clinical directorate level	84	Pathways at clinical directorate level	83	Formulation of objectives at clinical directorate level	73
Coherence training/strategic inputs	47	Clinical Audit	69	Compensation by objectives	47
Employee training database	46	Organizational rules at Clinical directorate level	51	Autonomy in defining strategies	46
		New professional figures and roles	51	Projects at clinical directorate level	27
		Certifications	15		

Source: Gabutti and Morandi 2018.

Three pairwise correlation analyses between the scores of couples of HRM families were then performed. This was done to understand whether there existed the tendency to privilege one or more families of practices at the expense of the others or whether, on the contrary, the tendency was to invest in each simultaneously. The analysis of coefficients revealed a positive association between each pair of dimensions. This suggested that they tend to be developed in parallel and that there may exist some favorable scenarios that globally encourage the development and implementation of innovative HRM practices in general.

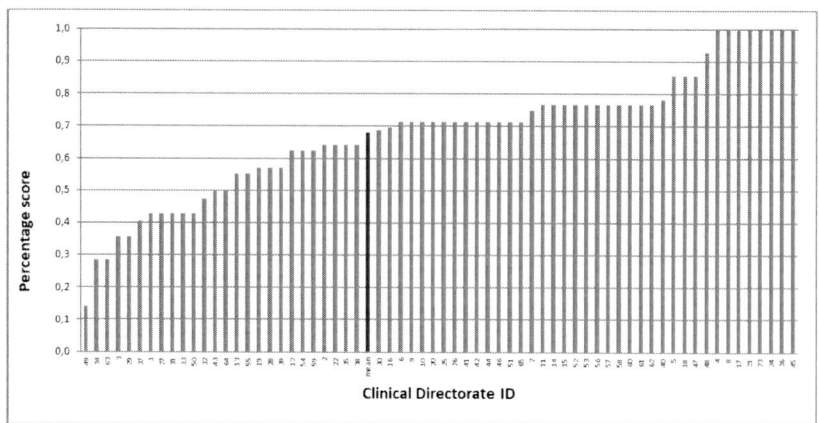

Source: Gabutti and Morandi 2018.

Figure 18. The score of clinical directorates in the implementation of training-related HRM tools.

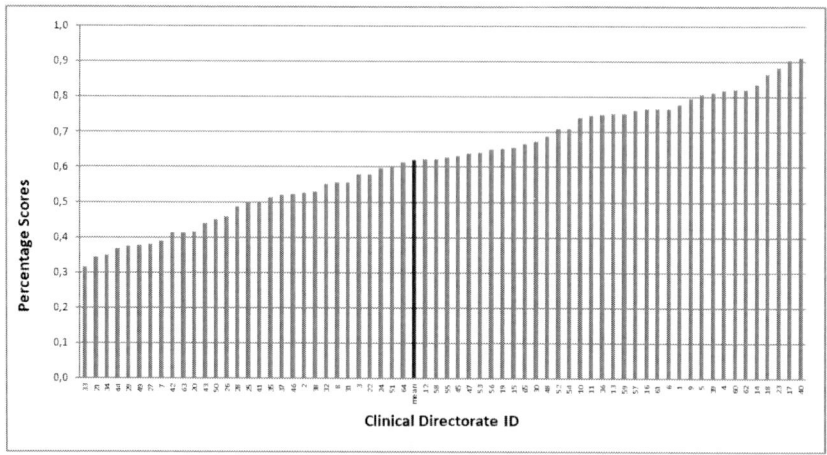

Source: Gabutti and Morandi 2018.

Figure 19. The score of clinical directorates in the implementation of control-related HRM tools.

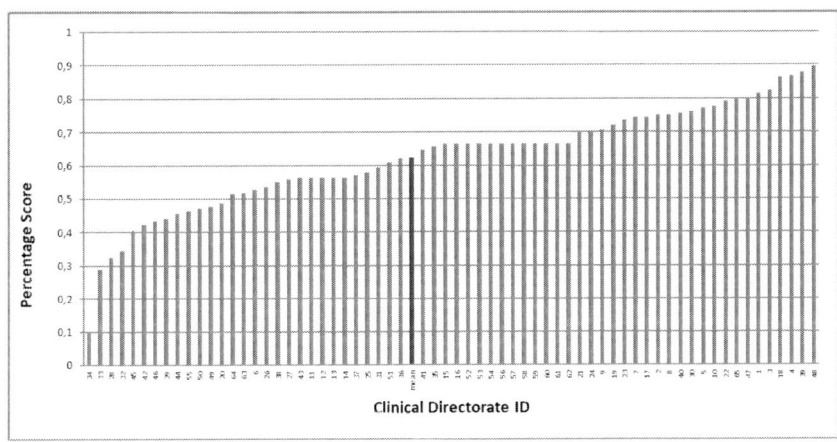

Source: Gabutti and Morandi 2018.

Figure 20. The score of clinical directorates in the implementation of objectives-related HRM tools.

The approach of this study is aimed at detecting the "infiltration level" of HRM tools in clinical directorates, to assess the degree to which they have concretely directed people's behaviors towards the objectives the clinical directorate model entails. This provides a vision of the tangible responsiveness of health care organizations to the model. The first point of interest has to do with a mean score of HRM tool implementation superior to 60% of a theoretical maximum, for each of the three families of tools analyzed. Whether this percentage is high or low is subject to interpretation. Clearly, a full implementation of the clinical directorate model through the use of HRM tools has not been detected. Yet, these percentages may indeed be considered satisfactory for various reasons. First because of the physiological distance there exists between ideality and feasibility. It is very unlikely to develop the "full set of HRM practices" which are coherent with the clinical directorate model because some might be inapplicable (e.g., because of the size of the organization, or of its mission) or might even be incoherent with the organization's strategy. The second reason why these percentages might be considered satisfactory has to do with the consideration that clinical directorates did not exist in Italy before the 1990s.

Although the study was carried out nearly two decades after their introduction, hospitals had to face drastic changes in their organizational assets, moving from centralized to decentralized configurations. This means that the shift towards the clinical directorate model had to start "from scratch" and it is well known that deep transformations in rooted features of complex organizations (as are HRM practices) frequently require many years to be implemented. Therefore, although not fully developed, these scores may indeed suggest a deep transformation in hospitals' daily functioning, in coherence with the model.

CONCLUSION

The success of each of the managerial aspects described in this book should be reconducted to their ability of contributing to the main dimensions of hospital performance. Any discrepancy between the performance desired and obtained should be quickly addressed through swift managerial interventions. It is not always obvious to develop a deep awareness of both the short- and long-term effects of managerial interventions in hospitals. The temptation to intervene through actions that may produce short-term desirable effects is frequently strong. Nevertheless, it is possibly dangerous to overlook the (intended and non-intended) effects of each single intervention in the longer run, which may or may not be coherent with the main strategies of change the hospital is trying to implement. In general, each one of the managerial fields described has the power to make a transition fail if not addressed adequately. In musical terms, each single item of the orchestra must play its part, or the overall symphony will just not sound right!

REFERENCES

Abrell-Vogel C and Rowold J 2014. "Leaders' commitment to change and the effectiveness in change- a multilevel investigation". *J Organiz Change Management; Vol. 27. Pages 900–921*

AlJaberi, O. A., Hussain M., and Drake P. R. 2017. "A Framework for Measuring Sustainability in Healthcare Systems." *International Journal of Healthcare Management*, 13:4, 276-285, doi: 10.1080/20479700.2017.1404710

Bravi, F., Gibertoni, D., Marcon, A., Sicotte, C., Minvielle, E., Rucci, P., Angelastro, A., Carradori, T., and Fantini, M. P. 2013. "Hospital Network Performance: A Survey of Hospital Stakeholders' Perspectives." *Health Policy* 109 (2): 150–57. https://doi.org/10.1016/J.HEALTHPOL.2012.11.003.

Brown, C. L., and Menec, V. 2018. "Integrated Care Approaches Used for Transitions from Hospital to Community Care: A Scoping Review." *Canadian Journal on Aging / La Revue Canadienne Du Vieillissement* 37 (2): 145–70. https://doi.org/10.1017/S0714980818000065.

Brown, C. L., and Menec,. 2021. "Measuring Processes of Integrated Care for Hospital to Home Transitions." *International Journal of Integrated Care* 21 (2). https://doi.org/10.5334/IJIC.5552.

Capolongo, S., Bottero, M. C., Lettieri, E., Buffoli, M., Bellagarda, A., Birocchi, M., Cavagliato, E., et al. 2015. "Healthcare Sustainability Challenge." *Green Energy and Technology* 218: 1–9. https://doi.org/10.1007/978-3-319-14036-0_1.

Carini, E., Gabutti, I., Frisicale, E. M., Di Pilla, A., Pezzullo, A. M., de Waure, C., Cicchetti, A., Boccia, S., and Specchia, M. L. 2020. "Assessing Hospital Performance Indicators. What Dimensions? Evidence from an Umbrella Review." *BMC Health Services Research* 20 (1): 1–13. https://doi.org/10.1186/s12913-020-05879-y.

Cowen, M., Halasyamani, L., McMurtrie, D., Hoffman, D., Volley, T., and Alexander, J. 2008. "Organizational Structure for Addressing the

Attributes of the Ideal Healthcare Delivery System." *Journal of Healthcare Management* 53 (6): 407–18.

Di Vincenzo, F. 2018. "Exploring the Networking Behaviors of Hospital Organizations." *BMC Health Services Research 2018 18:1* 18 (1): 1–10. https://doi.org/10.1186/S12913-018-3144-4.

Dizdar, Ö., Karadağ, Ö., Kalyoncu, U., Kurt, M., Ülger, Z., Çetinkaya Şardan, Y., and Ünal, S. 2007. "Appropriate Utilization of Hospital Beds in Internal Medicine: Evaluation in a Tertiary Care Hospital." *Journal of Evaluation in Clinical Practice* 13 (3): 408–11. https://doi.org/10.1111/J.1365-2753.2006.00724.X.

Dubas-Jakóbczyk, K., and Kozieł, A. 2020. "Towards Financial Sustainability of the Hospital Sector in Poland—A Post Hoc Evaluation of Policy Approaches." *Sustainability 2020, Vol. 12, Page 4801* 12 (12): 4801. https://doi.org/10.3390/SU12124801.

Gabutti, I., Mascia, D., and Cicchetti, A. 2017. "Exploring 'Patient-Centered' Hospitals: A Systematic Review to Understand Change." *BMC Health Services Research* 17 (1). https://doi.org/10.1186/s12913-017-2306-0.

Gabutti, I., and Morandi, F. 2018. "HRM Practices and Organizational Change: Evidence from Italian Clinical Directorates." *Health Services Management Research.* https://doi.org/10.1177/0951484 818790213

Güneş, E. D., and Yaman, H. 2017. *Health Network Mergers and Hospital Re-Planning.* Https://Doi.Org/10.1057/Jors.2008.165 61 (2): 275–83. https://doi.org/10.1057/JORS.2008.165.

Hartgerink, J. M., Cramm, J. M., Bakker, T. J. E. M., van Eijsden, R. A. M., Mackenbach, J. P., and Nieboer, A. P. 2014. "The Importance of Relational Coordination for Integrated Care Delivery to Older Patients in the Hospital." *Journal of Nursing Management* 22 (2): 248–56. https://doi.org/10.1111/J.1365-2834.2012.01481.X.

Herscovitch, L and Meyer J. 2002. "Commitment to organizational change: extension of a three component model". *J Appl Psychol Vol. 92, pages: 942–951.*

Koval, K. J., Chen, A. L., Aharonoff, G. B., Egol, K. A., and Zuckerman, J. D. 2004. "Clinical Pathway for Hip Fractures in the Elderly: The Hospital for Joint Diseases Experience." *Clinical Orthopaedics and Related Research*, no. 425: 72–81. https://doi.org/10.1097/01.BLO. 0000132266.59787.D2.

Liljas, A. E. M., Brattström, F., Burström, B., Schön, P., and Agerholm, J. 2019. "Impact of Integrated Care on Patient-Related Outcomes Among Older People – A Systematic Review." *International Journal of Integrated Care* 19 (3). https://doi.org/10.5334/IJIC.4632.

Maghsoudi, T., Cascón-Pereira, R. and Hernández Lara, A. B. 2020. "The Role of Collaborative Healthcare in Improving Social Sustainability: A Conceptual Framework." *Sustainability 2020, Vol. 12, Page 3195* 12 (8): 3195. https://doi.org/10.3390/SU12083195.

Schneider, M. A., and Pomidor, M. A. 2014. "The Value of a Progressive Care Environment for Neurosurgical Patients." *Journal of Neuroscience Nursing* 46 (5): 306–11. https://doi.org/10.1097/JNN. 0000000000000076.

ABOUT THE AUTHOR

Irene Gabutti is adjunct Professor in Organization Theory and Human Resource Management at the Catholic University in Rome, Italy. She is also a researcher at the Graduate School of Health Economics and Management (ALTMES), within the university. She is an economist by training and has obtained her PhD in Management and Public Health. She holds an over ten-year experience as a teacher and consultant in the healthcare management sector and has published numerous scientific articles in peer-reviewed journals.

While focusing on hospital organizational models and strategic management, she matured the belief that the complexity of these huge organizations makes it nearly impossible to drive change in a fully aware manner. However, it is on that single word *nearly* that she has built her research strategy.

Although she has frequently witnessed strong ambiguity and uncertainty in the environment in which hospital managers take their strategic decisions, she has grown confident that providing concrete guidance in driving organizational change in hospitals is indeed possible. It is in this spirit that she started working on practical toolkits and roadmaps aimed at increasing the awareness of hospital managers on the effects of their actions.

INDEX

A

activity-based costing, 47, 48, 91, 95
activity-based management, 47
ageing, 2, 12, 20, 102
allocating, xiii, 71, 72
ambulatory settings, 4
approach, viii, 6, 7, 23, 24, 25, 43, 44, 45, 46, 47, 48, 49, 50, 54, 59, 64, 68, 80, 81, 84, 91, 99, 102, 104, 110, 111, 118, 121, 125
attitudes, 34, 54, 70, 71, 88, 91

B

balanced scorecard, ix, 89, 103, 105, 106, 107, 110, 113, 116
Beveridge model, 8
Bismarck model, 8
bundled payments, 7

C

care, iv, vii, xii, 1, 3, 4, 5, 6, 8, 10, 11, 12, 13, 20, 21, 22, 23, 26, 28, 29, 30, 31, 36, 47, 54, 56, 58, 59, 65, 67, 68, 72, 74, 82, 84, 85, 86, 87, 88, 89, 91, 92, 93, 94, 95, 96, 98, 101, 102, 103, 108, 110, 111, 112, 113, 117, 118, 119, 121, 125, 127, 129
care manager, 67, 74
career ladder, viii, 60, 71, 81, 82, 83
career paths, 71, 81, 95
care-focused organizations, 21
chronic conditions, 20, 67, 91, 102
clinical data repositories, 63, 64
clinical directorate model, viii, ix, 15, 16, 17, 20, 21, 25, 119, 120, 125, 126
clinical directorates, xii, 15, 17, 18, 20, 26, 29, 30, 56, 57, 61, 64, 121, 122, 124, 125, 128
clinical directors, 17, 58, 76, 77, 80, 120, 121
clinical effectiveness, 101, 102
clinical pathways, xi, xii, 6, 12, 15, 23, 26, 33, 45, 47, 53, 56, 59, 102, 104, 107, 108, 110, 111, 118
clinical wards, xi, 17, 56, 62
compensation policies, 84

competencies, viii, xiii, xiv, 25, 33, 34, 36, 56, 57, 58, 60, 70, 71, 72, 75, 76, 77, 78, 79, 80, 81, 85, 89, 104, 119
competencies dictionary, 76
competency modeling, 75, 79, 81
comprehensive critical care model, 21
contextual characteristics, 52, 57
continuum of care, 5, 15, 20, 23, 63, 64, 68, 104, 106, 108, 118
core clinical processes, 24

D

day hospital, 4
day surgery, 4
decoupling, 30, 34, 35, 36, 40, 81, 93, 115, 120
departments, xi, xii, 15, 17, 18, 21, 24, 56, 58, 59, 60, 61, 82
directional control, 37

E

efficiency, xiii, 3, 7, 17, 21, 23, 24, 28, 56, 58, 69, 73, 101, 102, 104, 111, 112
electronic health records, 64, 88, 90
evaluating, xiii, 7, 71, 72, 98

F

fragmented care, 1, 5

G

goal ambiguity, 40, 86

H

heads of departments, 17

health technologies, xii, 36, 49, 50, 52, 53, 54, 55, 58, 59, 60, 85, 90, 98, 109, 118
health technology assessment, 33, 49, 50, 51, 52, 55, 85, 87, 98
health technology management tools, viii, 34, 48
healthcare systems, vii, 1, 2, 5, 6, 7, 8, 9, 10, 11, 28, 34, 63, 64, 67, 68, 93, 103, 109, 116, 127
hiring, xiii, 72, 89, 120
horizontal and transversal models, 21
hospital performance, ix, xiii, 3, 6, 9, 26, 33, 52, 55, 62, 69, 87, 99, 100, 101, 103, 104, 105, 106, 109, 110, 116, 126, 127
hospital-based health technology assessment, 49, 50, 51, 52, 90, 94
hospitals, vii, viii, ix, xi, xii, xiii, 1, 2, 3, 4, 6, 7, 9, 12, 13, 15, 16, 17, 18, 19, 20, 21, 23, 24, 25, 26, 27, 28, 29, 30, 33, 34, 35, 36, 39, 42, 43, 44, 45, 46, 47, 48, 49, 50, 52, 53, 55, 59, 61, 63, 65, 68, 69, 71, 72, 73, 74, 75, 76, 78, 79, 81, 85, 87, 88, 89, 90, 92, 96, 97, 99, 100, 102, 103, 104, 105, 106, 107, 108, 109, 111, 113, 115, 116, 117, 118, 119, 126, 128, 132
human resource management tools, 34

I

inappropriate settings, 3, 4, 24
information communication technology tools, viii, 34, 85
integrated approach, ix, 92, 115, 116
integrated care, 1, 5, 10, 11, 12, 13, 87, 90, 91, 93, 110, 127, 128, 129
intensity of care model, 21

J

job description, 76

K

key performance area, 105, 106, 107
key performance indicators, 105

L

liberal model, 8
long stay-low care, 22

M

management by objectives, 84
managerial accounting tools, viii, xii, xiv, 34, 37, 69, 84, 118
managerial career ladder, 82
managerial coherence, 115
multi-pathological, 2, 16, 20, 102
multi-professional teams, 22, 23, 33

N

new public management, 16, 17, 20, 28, 29, 30, 31, 116
non-core processes, 24

O

operational activities, 17
operative control, 37, 42
organizational charts, viii, xi, xii, 15, 16, 17, 25, 26, 27, 28, 33, 46, 61, 70, 76, 85, 115, 117
organizational models, viii, xii, 1, 15, 16, 19, 23, 25, 27, 35, 59, 65, 70, 72, 81, 115, 117, 132

P

patient-centered, viii, xiii, 5, 7, 15, 20, 23, 25, 26, 28, 29, 31, 48, 58, 64, 65, 72, 89, 102, 103, 104, 106, 113, 117, 128
patient-centered care, 5, 28, 31, 65, 72, 113
patient-centered model, 15, 23, 26
patient-centeredness, xiii, 58, 102, 103, 104, 106
performance dimensions, 9, 99, 104, 105, 109
primary care, 1, 3, 11, 92
professional career ladder, 82
professional roles, viii, 33, 70, 72, 74, 75, 76
progressive patient care model, viii, 15, 21, 23, 29

R

recovery plan, 66
responsive governance, 101, 102
role ambiguity, 74, 75, 86, 97
role conflict, 74, 75, 86, 97

S

safety, xiii, 11, 49, 65, 69, 88, 92, 95, 101, 102, 104, 106, 110
short-stay hospital, 22
staff orientation, 101
strategic partner, 40, 57, 70
strategic planning, 37
strategic plans, 17, 81, 93
strategy implementation, 81, 115
sustainability, 3, 7, 9, 10, 12, 19, 103, 108, 127, 128, 129

T

technology uptake, 52, 60
tertiary care, 1, 3, 128
timeliness, 68, 101
top management, 17, 26, 42, 54, 57, 58, 70, 73, 115
training, xiii, 54, 56, 57, 59, 68, 71, 72, 74, 80, 86, 94, 104, 107, 120, 121, 123, 124, 131

V

value, 44, 45, 46, 48, 99, 106, 108, 111, 112, 113, 122, 129

W

wards, 4, 17, 22, 24
week hospital, 4, 22
week surgery, 4, 74